Remember When

Remember When

Robert Mardle

Copyright © 2024 Robert Mardle

The moral right of the author has been asserted.

Apart from any fair dealing for the purposes of research or private study, or criticism or review, as permitted under the Copyright, Designs and Patents Act 1988, this publication may only be reproduced, stored or transmitted, in any form or by any means, with the prior permission in writing of the publishers, or in the case of reprographic reproduction in accordance with the terms of licences issued by the Copyright Licensing Agency. Enquiries concerning reproduction outside those terms should be sent to the publishers.

Troubador Publishing Ltd
Unit E2 Airfield Business Park
Harrison Road, Market Harborough
Leicestershire LE16 7UL
Tel: 0116 279 2299
Email: books@troubador.co.uk
Web: www.troubador.co.uk

ISBN 978-1-80514-271-3

British Library Cataloguing in Publication Data.
A catalogue record for this book is available from the British Library.

Printed and bound by CPI Group (UK) Ltd, Croydon, CR0 4YY
Typeset in 11pt Minion Pro by Troubador Publishing Ltd, Leicester, UK

To my friend, Michael

Contents

Introduction: Those Little Steps ix

1	A Bit of a Gamble	1
2	A Ton-Up Den	11
3	Carlos Fandango	19
4	Off to the Spa	24
5	Once Upon a Doughnut	32
6	Lawrence of Arabia	42
7	Avoiding Public Lavatories	48
8	Flying a Car	56
9	Och-Aye-Jimmy	64
10	A Life in the Toilets	75
11	Bankrupted Mini Monsters	83
12	To Ski or Not to Ski	93
13	All For One	100
14	Wrong Place and Wrong Time	108
15	Mai Tai's	116
16	In-Competent Crew	128
17	Come Fly with Me	135
18	Seniors Backpacking	141
19	My Dad Knew Nelson	152

20	A Bloke Called Padi	161
21	Living the Dream	166
22	King Richard	177
23	Strange Antiguan Customs	187
24	Golf – That Sinking Feeling	193
25	Indian Takeaway	200
26	A Christmas Party	213
27	Back to the Park	217
28	Crash-a-Lotti-Chef and Bike Rider	225
29	Who Needs Football?	238
30	Quins Cup Final	247
31	Harry's Football Team	252
32	Bullseye –Fifty Years	256
33	They Say It's All Over (West Ham 1966)	266

Introduction – Those Little Steps

My name is Robert Mardle and I'm successfully married to the old trouble and strife, Gail. Before putting a cork in it we had four children, Ben, Claire, Rebecca, and Thomas. I have written this book to prove to myself that even I can do it. After all, lots of other people have a go, so it can't be that difficult. Or so I thought! Using little snapshots and stories of my life would help give my family some more of an idea as to who I am and what I got up to.

I was hatched in 1950 at Wanstead hospital which wasn't far away from my dad who was also in hospital struggling with tuberculosis. Back in those days if you had TB, it was very serious. For the first two years of my life, I wasn't allowed to see him other than through the hospital's glass window. This was in case he passed it on to me. Once given the all-clear he was a weakened man having lost half his ribs and one lung to what is still, around the world, such a terrible disease. He had some catching up to do and so no sooner than he was home, surprise, surprise along came my little brother, John.

The first school I remember was Churchfields, across the road from where we lived in a block of flats at South Woodford. I remember going on my first day aged around five. It was very cold, frosty, and icy which was why we were wearing long socks. We kids were running and sliding down the pavement on the ice. Mrs Hollins, the head teacher, left her mark on me that day when she slapped me around the back of the legs. She was a right old bag. As is the way with these things, I don't think I ever got along with authority from that day on.

For our summer holidays we were woken up at 1.00am in the morning and bundled into the car. It was a very basic leftover post office van, and it was crammed full of necessities. I know my brother and I woke up fast, did what we were told and never argued. What didn't make it inside the car was tied onto the roof rack, and that was not somewhere you wanted to find yourself.

Off we went to Cornwall. Around the North Circular and down the A30 or the A303. It took until 5.00am by the time we had cleared East London and reached the still unfinished building site that is Stonehenge. Dad would have needed a pee break by then and the primus stove was lit, and on went the kettle for a brew.

John and I would have been very excited, and we were sent off to have a wee up against the ancient remains. What we never understood, and still don't, is why Stonehenge is such a big deal, for what we saw as being an unfinished building site. Remember, the Greeks and the Egyptians, a few thousand years earlier had actually built some things bigger, better, and certainly more useful. We can only tell you that if the ancient Brits had meant to build something to keep the sheep in, they failed. The bloody things are all over the place because they didn't bother to finish the job or put the bloody doors on.

After we had finished climbing up and down the ancient stones, we were encouraged to have a 'kip' before the journey was resumed. For us, the original wild west pioneers, after the rocks, the first big hurdle was a well-known problem back in those days. The legend and challenge that was "Okehampton

Hill". You have to remember that at that time of year, the whole of post-war London was on its way to the West Country. The cars were very basic. Three-speed gearboxes, vacuum driven windscreen wipers that didn't really work in the rain, and brakes that only worked when you didn't use them. The traffic jams were the things of legend. Too make those people that stayed at home feel good, the chaos featured on the evening news every weekend. Some of the problem was that if you weren't driving along with the air flowing through and cooling the radiator, cars like ours just boiled over and quickly overheated. For this reason dad, having been in the war, used to carry lots of spare water in Jerry cans strapped onto the side of the car. They got their name because they were cheap, made by the losing side and left over from the war.

Eventually, along with hundreds of other cars, we would reach the top of the Okehampton mountain and then start the descent. That's when the car brakes, with the added weight of the water cans, the entire contents of our flat and with four passengers, would start to overheat. Drivers were encouraged to take emergency detours into nearby farmer's fields when things went out of control. This wasn't all so bad as the ever-enterprising Cornish, by then, had given up tin mining and invented pasties and clotted cream teas. In triumph we would eventually get to the end of the A30 at around 4.00pm, fifteen or sixteen hours after leaving Woodford on the east side of London. That's when the real holiday would begin.

I think I took in and learned more than my school reports suggested. Some of our teachers, those that you liked and learned from, were really good. The others just threw blackboard rubbers at you. We had to take exams aged eleven. These would decide if you passed and went to a nice posh grammar school or were just rubbish and failed. Failure was when you got sent off to a government approved, overcrowded, and underfunded secondary modern school. What was good about them was they did at least give you a free school meal every day, which I always loved.

I went to the big school for failures where for the first two years we were sent to an annexe three miles away from the main school. To begin with we caught the bus and eventually I was allowed to ride my bike. This worked fine until the big smog of the early sixties which was caused by burning coal. The pollutants combined with moisture to become a fog that was really very dangerous to breathe. You really couldn't see. Visibility was down to four or five feet, and you had to wrap a wet towel over your mouth to breathe. There were no bikes and no buses. It was a long and dangerous way to walk to school.

We would go shopping to the butchers, the greengrocers, the baker and so on. Lipton's were the grocers and that was where you went for all your dry goods which would be measured out to order for you by the person behind the counter. Sure, you got packets of tea, butter, and some other key lines. Bulk ingredients – rice, flour, biscuits, sugar, cheese and the like – were individually weighed out for you into a paper bag. The shops were closed Wednesday and Saturday afternoons as well as all day Sunday. Now for me, wouldn't it be nice if we did some of that again these days?

For 6d (sixpence) we went to Saturday morning cinema put on for a mixed age group of eight- to twelve-year-olds. We had great black and white episodes of *Flash Gordon* and *Roy Rogers*. The first Chinese restaurant we ever saw opened across the road from where we lived. In 1963 and for 7/6d (seven shillings and sixpence), you got the number one set menu. Shark fin soup, sweet and sour pork, special fried rice, and special Chicken Chow-Mein noodles. Apart from the price, not much has changed there then.

If, when you got home your mum was out, you used to be able to climb up the drainpipe on the outside of our block of flats. We were on the third floor and had to be:

a) Careful not to fall down or:
b) Tread on Timothy our pet tortoise who lived on the balcony.

He was a mad bugger. He often tried to fly, and we used to find him three floors down, on the grass, happily munching away.

We learned to ride bikes in the gardens of our flats. There was a hill between the block of flats at the top of the estate, and the ones down at the bottom. To begin with you got on your bike at the top and just let go. You fell off and crashed a few times, but you couldn't let on that it hurt, and so you quickly got the hang of that. Then there was no stopping us, and we learned to ride like dare devils all around the trails of Epping Forest.

Epping forest was huge and was a forerunner to islands of adventure. You learned to climb really high up into the big trees. Ride and jump ditches and ramps on your bikes. Make dens, hideaways in the bushes, that honestly you could have lived in. It was where you tried smoking cigarettes, which in the day, you could actually buy in packets of five from the corner shop. I remember clearly the winters were so cold and we had lots of snow. In the summer it was the opposite, long days and very hot. We would be up playing on the edge of the forest and for "fun" set fire to some bushes. The big deal was watching the fire engine come rushing out and do its thing.

Whenever the weather was good, our fathers were great in organising football and cricket games for all the boys, in the park. We didn't seem to spend a lot of time indoors. We were happy playing around on bomb sites, climbing trees, and making camps in the back of someones nearby orchards. In the summer we would go every day to 'the Kingfisher' swimming pool for the whole day. Mum, before going to work, would make us sandwiches and for 3d (which was three pence or a threepenny bit) you could buy a Wagon Wheel chocolate biscuit at lunchtime. It's worth noting that in those days, you needed two hands to hold and eat one of these monsters. Nowadays you get five "bite sized" excuses in a bag for £1.50p. Progress, hmmm!

On the way home you could go to the bakers and ask for a penny's worth of stale buns. If you got lucky, they would off-load the previous day's unsold cakes and buns which weren't really stale. The other one was to go to the chip shop and ask for the batter shavings. A bag full of super tasty and greasy bits of batter that had broken away during the cooking process.

Aged eleven I had a paper round which was hard work. There was no mucking about. Mr Wetherill was the strict owner of a newsagents across the road and my mother worked there. During the week, at 7.00am I delivered newspapers and magazines to a hundred houses each day, before school. They were heavy and you had this great big canvas bag that felt like it was twice your size. On Sundays it was a killer and you had to take two bags and split the round. The worst part was trying to get all this newsprint through people's tiny, little, letterboxes. The tips at Christmas were good! On Saturday mornings, after the paper round, I had a job at a wood furniture makers operating a bandsaw. When you got it right it made legs for chairs. When I got it wrong it made sawdust which, as Mr Cody an ex-wartime sergeant major, would say wasn't much Fxxxin good for anything.

On Friday nights there was Boy Scouts, which I loved. The 52nd Epping Forest used to meet, and we played games and learned to do basic stuff like tie knots, sew on buttons and light a fire. Once every year our founder, Baden Powell, said we had to do good in the community. He was clearly thinking of me with this idea of his. He called it Bob a Job Week. Being a Robert, everyone called me Bob at this point in my life. It was kind of weird when you knocked on people's front doors and said my name was Bob. That I was asked to do any job they wanted doing for a shilling, which in old speak was known as a Bob. I ended up knocking myself out for next to nothing, cleaning people's cars, cutting their grass and doing their gardening, which I still hate to this day. Baden Powell never thanked me personally, but I worked hard and raised quite a few Bob for him, so that he could continue to live very well. They even made him a Lord for all 'his' hard work and his fondness for helping young boys.

The best of the jobs I had was to do Mrs Kite's shopping. She would give me the shopping list and off I would go and get it all for her. She lived on the fourth floor above us, and I think she had the hots for our dad. Even if he was interested, which I don't think he was, he was too knackered. He had spent the whole week driving a converted, war-time Bren gun carrier come post office van, all over the south of England. My brother and I thought she looked like Cruella de Ville, with the make-up the hairdo and long, painted fingernails. We thought she was a vampire. She lived in the dark and kept all the curtains drawn and never went out in the sunshine. She kept closely in touch with us by paying me 10/- (ten shillings a week) to do her bidding.

Because of our dad's success with his hard work, my parents moved from East London to Gosport on the South Coast. In London, I was actually happy at school with my mates, all the mischief, and the part time jobs. I suppose life was always going to change and at age fourteen I had to give it all up, move schools and start over. It was never the same again. I was tall, not from the area, and I stood out which meant people picked on me. I had to stand up for myself to fit in which wasn't easy and it kept getting me into trouble. The schoolwork was different, and I found myself either in front of the subject or behind on it.

My mum had taken a job as a school dinner lady, and this made it a bit awkward. Mr Duncan, the deputy headmaster, was a bit too fond of giving me six of the best. He looked a lot like Adolf Hitler, and we all thought he was probably related to him. The flogging was enthusiastically delivered to your bum with either the sole of a rubber boot or just the wooden cane. I had rather a lot to do with him. Mr Penny the headmaster was a much nicer man and got along well with my mother. He found himself in a very difficult spot when he had to keep asking mum why I wasn't at school.

Aged fifteen I had by now discovered my best new friends, Willy, girls and the Mocambo coffee bar with its juke box and football table. This was when, for me, it all started to come apart. Being quite big and looking older than I was, I began to hang out and get along with blokes who were older than me and had scooters and jobs.

One day I remember shooting at crows (I hate crows) with an air rifle, somewhere out the back of our house. Some bloke came over to me and claimed I was shooting at him. I was cocky and not so little and said, "so what. What are you going to do about it" I was holding the gun and felt that I had the upper hand in that situation. Out of nowhere, as fast as you can imagine, he just punched me hard on the nose and I fell down, beaten and bleeding. It hurt and that was a good lesson to have learned early in adult life.

The reality was that I was well brought up by mum and dad, with good manners and encouraged to speak nicely. Despite being in classes of fourty five pupils, I had taken note of what was important at school and learned stuff. Secondary school drummed it into you and taught me to spell, do all the basics of maths well and definitely the times tables. I was thrown out aged fifteen, and then again aged sixteen when I was went to catering school. For a few years I bumped around a lot, wasting my time and going nowhere. I was just a typically ignorant, inexperienced idiot with no idea and no imagination.

The first record I ever bought was a 45rpm single, *Return to Sender*. First 33rpm long-playing record was Elvis Presley's *GI Blues*.

The first time I flew in an aeroplane was aged twenty-one going on our honeymoon, on a packaged trip to Majorca in 1971.

The first grubby X rated film I went to see was, Irma La Duce, at the Odeon cinema in George lane. I was and must have looked fourteen. The lady at the ticket desk asked how old I was. I said eighteen. The film wasn't at all grubby and that was a waste of money. Another good lesson in life, learned.

There came a time in 1979 when trying to get my own business of the ground, I upgraded my Ford Cortina and moved on up to a whole new level. A giant step, Dagenham dustbin to Deutsche Munich, with a quality six-cylinder BMW on alloy wheels. It had an electric aerial that went up and down. When you turned on the state-of-the-art Pioneer radio, two surface mounted speakers delivered the best sound yet. It had a cassette player and we played very loud Lionel Ritchie and Billy Joel tracks which, fourty five years on, we still play today. We've bought decent quality cars ever since.

We had bought our first Sony colour TV in 1978. It took two people to lift it. We had a VHS, not Betamax, video recorder. We could now tape programmes off the TV to play back later. We could then buy or hire feature films on tape from the video shop.

I bought my first computer for work in the early 1980s. It was an ACT computer running Sirius software on two floppy discs. In one drive you had a disc with the programme on. In the other drive the data. These things quickly evolved, and the funny thing was we continued with the guys who developed the software, and used their programmes to run our business, right up until 2010.

In 1981, aged 31, I bought my first Porsche 911. It was fitted with an in-car telephone and a huge wobbly aerial that came out of the window and was suction stuck to the roof. You asked an operator to connect you to the number and pressed the transmit button to talk and released it to listen. If that wasn't bad enough, the first mobile phone was a Motorola. The battery weighed in at eight pounds and you carried it in one hand. The phone itself was the size of a brick and weighed three pounds. Exhausted, you carried that in the other hand.

In 1985 we all bought Sony Walkman portable cassette players. Groundbreaking little headphones and fantastic sounds directly into your ears. We still had vinyl records, but this was the real start of the digital revolution. With cassette tapes you recorded your own music which became even easier when write your own CDs came along. Things by this time were changing and developing very quickly. Tapes had this annoying habit of getting tangled up. CDs didn't and replaced the original vinyl records and record players. Before you knew it someone had invented the MP3 players and iPods which were the size of a packet of Five Woodbine cigarettes. They would store hundreds of CDs which you could sort and organise to suit yourself.

It's been truly memorable trying to write this book. It's made me look back and remember all the stuff I did and some of the scrapes I got into. I think it's taken me a long time to grow up, but I got there in the end. There was never a plan and I seem to have gone through life, flying by the seat of my pants and by just taking it all in my stride. What they call good luck is I believe just how you react to opportunities. The decisions you then make, good or bad and how they open the door to the next round of options!

Looking back, I have no idea how any of this happened. What I do know is meeting Gail, my wife, being accepted by her father, brother and friends really helped put me on my feet. I owe them more than I realise. Making our own family gave a real purpose to our lives. It was always expensive and, with some little people to care for, fight for, and protect, I had to work very hard and to keep pushing forwards.

It showed me what could be done and forced me to get on and do it. The result is that it has turned out to have been a lot of fun, mostly good decisions which in the end:

**For a Toilet Roll Salesman,
has all turned out really quite well.**

A Bit of a Gamble

What we all take for granted is that, pretty much every day, this lovely person, in shorts and workwear, puts a letter through the letterbox in your front door. It just sits there waiting for us, at our leisure, to come and pick it up. What a great service.

Anyways, one day, through the post, I received this letter from HMRC. Unbelievably it said, Her Majesty the Queen had decided to give me loads of money, every week and forever more until death do us part. This great news, however, was sort of expected. When it does actually happen it's just amazing, like it's free money. I have had a £1 premium bond since I was aged ten. I've still got it and what a waste that turned out to be. It created loads of expectation, hope as well as disappointment. What it hadn't done was to win me any money, which of course was the whole idea. Now apparently, I had been chosen by the government and was going to be given free money forever.

The only times in my life that I have ever gambled is when I've got completely carried away or had too many drinks. That said there was the time in 1980 when I

was on my way back from the Royal Victoria pub in Binfield. The Hammers, West Ham, were in the football cup final. They were playing another north London club, Arsenal, otherwise known as the 'Gunners'. We lived in Binfield at that time and there was a bookies shop near to the baker and the candlestick makers. I was never sure about football in those days. When I was younger and on a few occasions my cousins had taken me to see the 'Hammers". They were, for some strange reason, always blowing bubbles at Upton Park their home ground. That wasn't my first football game of course. My dad, it turned out, liked football, shooting big guns, and driving crazy vehicles. It follows then that he was a 'Gunners' supporter.

Back in the early days of the war he had been given an armoured vehicle with a big Bren gun fixed on the front. I should imagine he thought he was Dennis Top Dog. As private gunner he had to do as he was told, which was to look out for anyone named Jerry. In fact, come to think of it, I also remember him telling me how as a young soldier, having just left the school for aspiring monks, he had  joined the army. He was trained and then posted to an airfield at Hainault in Essex. His job was to fire this great big anti-aircraft gun up into the sky keeping everyone safe from this same bloke called Jerry.

Back in those days the post office was amazing as well as very important. Obviously, they were very busy posting service personnel all over the world. I'm not sure how they ever got them through the letter box. They probably just knocked on the door and handed them over. Then a bit like a recorded delivery, you had to sign for them. How different it is these days! To this day, if ever you go over to Hainault, do take a moment to look around.

You will notice how good our dad was. Fifty years on and there are very, very few pigeons flying around, and no one called Jerry.

It sort of follows then that my dad, having played with all those guns, would naturally become an Arsenal supporter. It was he and Uncle Alf who took me to see my first division one football game. I really can't remember who Uncle Alf was, but I do recall he was a nice bloke, worked with Dad and that we did all go to his wedding.

The Arsenal home ground was mostly made of wood, painted in red and cream colours. Probably, post-war times being hard, it was paint scrounged from the Great Western & London North-Eastern railways that ran nearby. Even then, a season ticket to football was very desirable and beyond the reach of most booking hall clerks. In those days, if you knew who to ask, a ticket for the year could get you an awful lot of free paint.

Above the main red/cream grandstand, which looked very suspiciously like a ten-carriage Pullman train, was a proud symbol of Arsenal's heritage, an Army horse drawn field gun.

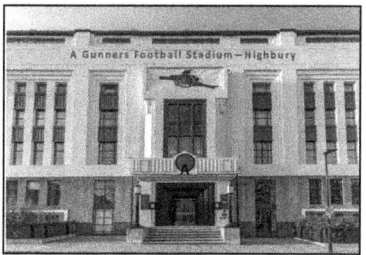

Back then, when I was growing up you were expected to participate in playground conkers, football, and cricket. Let's face it, most of us were rubbish at all of them. That didn't matter as long as you played conkers and chose to support a football team. You chose your team and, always and forever, stuck with them.

In the 1950s you could get arrested for being naughty, breaking the peace, farting in public or just being a little drunk and disorderly. The arresting policeman would ask, "what's your name son?" followed by the age-old question, "and who do you support?" The right answer would see you walk free (if you could, that is). If you were rich and could count to ten backwards, then a police car would kindly drive you home. You see football is more than just a game, it defines you and who you are. Once you chose your team, you stuck with them and followed them. It was bad practice to change teams, and I never did.

As we have become older and started travelling the world it's amazing. What was once our national game has become such a big deal around the whole world. You can get off a long-haul flight to say, Cambodia or Timbuktu, go outside the airport and climb into a beaten-up taxi or a tuk-tuk. The driver is usually wearing an old, very faded football team shirt. The first thing they would say to you is, "Where you from?" We reply of course, "England". The next thing said, in broken taxi-driver English, is who he supports. Usually, Chelsea or Manchester United. Then he looks at you and asks, "Who you support?" As a bloke I of course have to say that I still support West Ham. This usually gets a wobble of the head and a genuinely big smile that says, well somebody has too.

Then I trot out some names, Bobby Moore, Jeff Hurst, Trevor Brooking, Gordon Banks and of course Frank Lampard and his dad Frank Lampard Snr. Even in the Punjab they have heard of the game's legends. All these players have at one time, or another played for both England and the Hammers.

On a serious note. It hit home to me a way back, the global importance of sport and how it brings us ordinary people together. Wherever you go around the world, with sport, you can instantly strike up a conversation with say the pool attendant, the waiter or barman. In fact, we like wandering around in different countries. Often ending up in local street markets where you can so easily become the centre of attention.

I think it's about my being so much taller than most of us foreigners. We both stand out having blue eyes and Gail, who is a curly blonde. Young men can and do often gather around and start asking you questions. It's genuine interest, although we are always very careful. We don't wear expensive watches, bags, or bling. We only take out things we need, keeping cash in a shoe and a little, get out of jail cash, in a buttoned-down pocket just in case.

I suppose I'm OK at getting people to relax and to laugh. Football and cricket are the two games that always seem to get everyone going. They will always ask of course, "What team do you support" and off we go. Most of the time I know nothing

about what I'm saying but it is fun. In that moment and for that short time we are all enthusiastic friends and are as one. It's often so amazing seeing how poor people can appear to be, however, when it comes to it, they all have mobile phones, TVs and how knowledgeable they are.

My team, West Ham, beat Arsenal winning the cup that weekend in 1980. I won forty quid; it was real and proper gambling. You went into the grubby little betting shop. Everyone smoked, the walls and ceilings were nicotine stained which was quite normal back then. You put your money on the counter and said what your forecast was. The person behind the security bars, who was also probably smoking, gave you a small receipt. It was all cash since credit cards hadn't been invented at that point in time. Because of the cash, bank robbing and knocking over bookies shops was still a very popular past time back then. Fortunately, I was still too young to give it a go.

With a good result, you went back to the little shop. You acted like a 'Joe Cool Dude' who did this all the time. You would swagger up to the barred window and the person, who was still sitting inside, smoking a fag, took your little betting slip and then they give you back your winnings, and nothing gets said. I don't remember anyone smiling or wishing you a nice day, that's not how it works. It's just a betting shop! The best bit about all this was it was cash, and my wife Gail didn't know I had it. Things were so much nicer back then.

Another example of my reckless gambling was on our first trip on a cruise boat, the QE2 to New York. This was of course in the good old days when the QE2 was of course the Queen Elizabeth 2. Its now been renamed the Queen Camilla and sold to the Arabs. My wife Gail and I were 'poshing it up' and dressed up like Christmas Trees. We would have had champagne aperitifs in the Tattinger bar. Dinner was in the Princes Grill along with a glass or two of fine vintage wine. You do end up getting a bit carried away and get sucked into the whole experience. You're all made up, feeling, and acting very cool. Full of 'bonhomie' and French wine, you toddle off to the casino, better known as the den of dreams.

Now that's a scary experience. Everyone else clearly knows what they are doing, and we do not. It's as quiet as a church. You stroll around the lush, expensive looking room avoiding eye contact with everybody and anybody. It's all so serious and nobody actually looks like they're having any fun! Not many people talk. It's sort of like one of those big art auctions. Punters just sit there, on their own, flicking their fingers

or nodding their heads to indicate they want to 'go again'. OK, so there are the odd exceptions. Some people do seem normal and like us, look to be enjoying themselves. Despite our trying to be cool, everyone can tell we are 'casino virgins'. You can't help but feel everyone is looking at you and measuring you up. They smile at you and so being polite we end up talking to them. We then feel terrible since perhaps we're upsetting their karma. Really the opposite is probably true as it gives them a chance to come back to the real world. Instead of casually pushing piles of their money chips around the table they get to take a breather. Anyway, we are certainly extremely impressed.

We're brave and we don't want to let on that 'we have no idea' so we watch and learn. We go to the cashier's desk and ask for £100 of chips, without salt or vinegar I said, jokingly. That didn't go down very well! Now we're committed and we must have a go. We're quite sweet really. For a hundred quid all you get is just ten chips. Gail gets half and I get the other five. They look strangely like something magical from the land of Lego. OK, it's time and I'm always the one to jump in first and so we have a go. Well, someone has to!

Fully loaded and having cased the joint, we find the roulette table with, we think, the friendliest looking croupier. With what we've seen and heard, I go for it. I tell myself to take it easy and don't rush, be cool. One chip £10 on both red and evens. Well, my favourite number is two and that's evens. The nice lady from the Philippines with lots of makeup and sticky-on eyelashes, spins the wheel. I look at her and smile nicely. It stops on black number 21. Hmm! I look at Gail and she giggles showing me that she has still got more chips than me.

No worries on my part, I've played before. Sure, that was just beginner's bad luck, right? I smile at Barbie and go again with the same choice, red and evens. Launching the ball, she's being extra careful not to break a nail. That would of course be bad luck but I'm not sure who for at this point in my gambling career. The all-important ball deliberately jumps and bumps around in order to create some kind of excitement. We see it it's settling, it's looking good, it's almost on red, it's almost on 24. Then the bloody thing hiccups stopping on black 17 and there goes another tenner.

Meanwhile, Gail has, of course, worked out what I'm doing wrong. Reassuringly I tell her that it's "great fun" and that she should get into "the game". She asks Filipino Barbie, the roulette policewoman, who smiles and says, "sure you can put your chip at the very bottom of a whole column." Gail, who has been tottering around on 6" high heels, has now worked out she can reach that far, has a 3:1 chance (better than my 50:50) and she goes for it. Now, I know that I am an experienced and successful toilet roll salesman. I may be cautious, but I am street wise. I stick with it on 50:50. I've lost twice, so with caution back on the red and evens.

The over excited ball gets launched again while Barbie looks up at the ceiling. Maybe she's embarrassed, having trouble with the stick-on nails or just plain bored. We don't know and we huddle together giggling. Plink, plinky, plink goes the soppy ball. Finally, it stops on Red 14. You would think West Ham had won the cup again! As the excitement settled and we stopped grinning, Barbie gives Gail three chips and me only two. I quickly realise that Gail is now 2 chips up and I'm still one chip down. I think this then, is the trouble with Gambling. We start getting adventurous and I need to go bold. Having noticed that this table has all the action between numbers 13 and 24, the

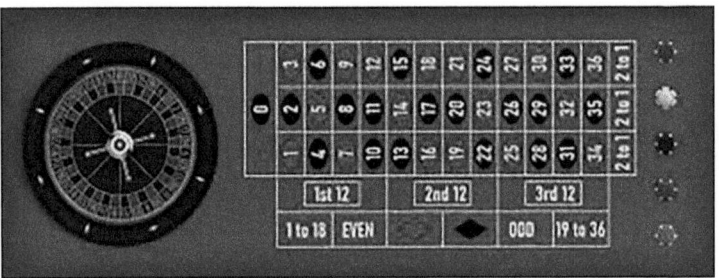

middle of the board is the place to be. Like a seasoned gambler I "double down" This is an odd saying when you're actually raising the stakes? I now put *two* of my very expensive Lego chips down on where the action is, Red 24.

Gail stays where she is and puts her by now, very warm chip at the bottom of a whole column. It's right in the middle of the table, which is where she can still reach. The wheel goes around one way and the plinky plonky ball goes the other. Barbie stares at the mirrored ceiling where she can still see herself. Low and behold, as Joseph once said to Mary, it's turned out well. Bang in the middle, an even number 32. Barbie who is lightning fast at taking and giving, snatched my £10 chip away whilst chanting something about Red 32. Gail on the other hand received another three chips back again. She was now up by forty pounds, and I was down another tenner.

Well, we were 'in it to win it' so we crashed on. Gail smartly went for a family grouping of numbers one to six. I went for my lucky number two. This time Barbie used a new ball, which I wasn't happy about. The Casino always wins right? Plinky, Plonk and Bosh, it only came up as number six. Gail now needed a bigger bag, and I was down to my last two Lego chips.

Even though my brains running flat out, I work out that this table is now stuck and running on even numbers. Dressed like a penguin I was getting hot. What do I do next? Gail, ever the calm one, was playing like an old pro. She placed her next chip on a corner covering both my number as well as another lucky family number which for her was four. I boldly went all in with my last two chips. I followed Gail's earlier triumphs, at the bottom of the column, using my lucky number which is two. Let's go I thought to myself.

Same old stuff as before. The wheel goes round and round. The ball still makes funny blinky, blonky noises and the tension builds. You try to look smooth and realise you're no longer breathing and that you are clenching your bottom cheeks tightly.

When it all stops it's hard to believe. It only goes and lands on number four and I'm done. I've lost everything. The banks are going to repossess the house, take the car and the children will have to go to a state school.

On the other hand, Gail's gone and won the lottery. Barbie, whose probably really a man, shoves over a stack of Lego chips and even smiles. We looked around the room expecting applause, but no one seemed to have noticed. Gail, her little bag now bulging with £10 Lego chips, wants to quit and go back to our suite to count her money.

It's a funny old world and how gambling brings out the worst in people. What started out as "Our Money" had so quickly and stealthily moved across the invisible marital divide and became her money. It was never to be mentioned and certainly not to be seen by me again. I followed Gail and her bulging bag, to the door. The security man saw us back to our suite, giving me an understanding goodnight pat on the shoulder as we went back into our suite.

Gail was very impressed and wants to go again tomorrow.

A Ton-Up Den

As I think back, I realise my dad was a hero, an amazing man and a great father. He was always dependable, reliable, and solid. Despite all his own problems, he never gave up on me. I now understand that as you get older and wiser it's normal to regret all the important things that you didn't do. I kick myself for being so wrapped up in myself, my work, and my family. For not having spent more time talking with him as he got older and struggled everyday with his health. It's too late now.

We are after all the products of our upbringing. The basic groundwork and how we are brought up is all done by our parents, our homelife and then our schooling. It's important to remember how much he had to do with who we are now, and the people we have become.

My dad once told me how he had escaped from the church's priesthood academy by enlisting into the army during the war. After he had learned to shoot people, fight, crawl through muddy drains and attack bags filled with straw he became an elite army commando. These were specialised, small units of  the army who got to do difficult stuff. He liked driving Bren gun carriers and shooting big guns, hmm? His unit was sent on a raid at the occupied french port of Dieppe. It was intended to destroy the German submarine docks.

This attack went horribly wrong. He was injured when an explosion threw him into a wall. He maintains it was the force of this explosion that triggered the illness. The tuberculosis was already in his body, and this then triggered his lifelong fight with the disease. The army discharged him on medical grounds.

In 1950 surgery removed half his lungs, some ribs, and hung him upside down to dry out. He somehow miraculously survived, continued smoking senior service cigarettes, and still found time to make me!

In the 1950s our parents had a really tough time. Dad was very ill spending nearly two years in the hospital. During that time my mum was supported closely by her family. It was my Uncle Harry, and mum's sister, Auntie May, who stepped in for dad whilst he was struggling to get better. Buses cost money and we didn't have any. So, every Tuesday I was made to walk the four miles to our nan's, with my mum and our dog called Rex. After Jerry had bombed their home in London's Docklands, they had been forced to move out to a house at Sheere Road in Barkingside.

I can still remember what a lovely, crazy place this was. Mum's was a big family of ten. They had a cocky spaniel dog called Sally and very tasty chickens whose names are long forgotten, and a rabbit. They all seemed to live here in the one small house with an outside toilet and one tin bath. On a good day, Nan would give my mum sixpence so we could catch the bus back home.

Dad never made a fuss. He worked hard as he got better and stronger although, because of his TB, people were reluctant to employ him. He was calm, thoughtful, and avoided confrontations wherever possible. He was always great to talk to and his biggest skill was to listen carefully. Everyone liked him.

On reflection, I now think he really loved driving, had a liking for speed and a passion for hot cars. As a passenger, he never flinched when my brother or I were doing silly things racing up and down roads in record times. He eventually found himself a decent job in the 1960s. Starting as a sales rep he travelled around in all sorts of cars, selling aluminium foil and containers to the food industry. The company car was a British Racing Green, Ford Zephyr Six. It won't mean much to you, but at the time, it was super cool to me and my brother. It was big and had sticky up tail fins. It would seat six people. Three on the front bench seat and three in the back. It had a column gear change and the speedo read 120mph.

One of Dad's specialties was to come home from work and

take all four of us around the North Circular Road to the famous Staples Corner. This was where all the 'ton-up boys' hung out at the Ace of Spades café. Lots of chewing gum, motorbikes, leather jackets and jeans. This was also where the M1, Britain's first motorway, started. It ran forty-six miles to a petrol station at Newport Pagnell where the builders had run out of money. At the end there was a collection box and drivers were invited to put some money in it. This was so they could build some more of this fabulous road, all the way to Birmingham and to the rest of the UK.

Back in the day there were no speed limits on major roads and petrol was 4/8p a gallon. That's 24 pence in today's speak. To be fair, most cars of that time had three speed gearboxes and top speeds of 60/70mph. British Race car builders like Aston Martin and Jaguar would test their Le Mans sports cars up and down the M1, this wonderful, newly built drag strip of a road. There were no speed limits back then. They were of course all road legal having mudguards, windscreen wipers, and lights. They reached speeds of nearly 200mph, down the M1, in the middle of the night. This proved their durability and speed over the forty-six miles. It didn't take them long. When they got to the end of the new M1, to avoid the road works, and the collection box, they braked really hard, turned around and just went back the other way. They went on to beat the world.

As boys we loved it and knew what was coming as we passed the Ace of Spades. We would sit in the back of the 'Zephyr 6' and Dad would give it some welly whilst we would egg him on to the magic Ton (100mph) At the time it was all perfectly normal. There was no oxygen. There were no seat belts, no air bags and not many other things that would make a car safe. We thought we were like Flash Gordon travelling at the speed of light. Dad would get the ton-up. We would all cheer and then, with the job done, gradually slow down and light up a Senior Service smoke.

Meanwhile, blokes on motorbikes with names like the Dunstall Dominator, Silver Bullet and the Norton Commando would continue to roar past us as we were slowing down. The riders were otherwise known as Greasers or Rockers. They would be crouched over the petrol tanks, desperately clinging on. Some didn't wear crash helmets, and some wore leathers like their track idols and champions Mike Halewood and John Surtees.

We all have a shoe box under the bed. In my 'box in the cupboard' I found a race ticket from Goodwood back in the 1960s. Dad, who was then in his forties, had taken us all to a motor race featuring all the big names of the time. This would have been around the time  of Stirling Moss, Mike Hawthorne, and Jack Brabham. Looking back, I realise now, that we were always going to motorbike speedway evenings and stock car events. I'm not clear as to how my brother and I came to be obsessed with cars, but I think our dad had probably something to do with it.

I bought my first car, a Ford Poplar 103E, in 1966. At that time, I was living in a shared house in Gosport. My mother had had enough of me and to be fair so had the school and catering college. I was working in a factory welding radiators together. What was so funny was that there was little or no control over the expensive and sophisticated materials used to make them. You just went and got what you needed to get from the stores. The precious metals were necessary to braze the metal tubes together. This was  stuff like phosphorous, magnesium and the like. So, by doing the job well, being careful every day you could end up with a roll of very expensive metal left over.

When not actually working on the job, we all waddled around in our Dickies boilersuits. With both our hands stuck inside the side pockets we looked like a flock of waddling penguins. At lunch times everyone waddled off to the pub which was perfectly normal. No one actually drank alcohol in those days and of course, being under eighteen, it was against the law. The pub, however, did great cheese and onion rolls which to this day, along with cheese and onion crisps, are still my favourites.

Douggie was my mentor and had helped me get a job at the factory. He showed me that there were one or two scams going on, which I should be aware of. The laundry switch on Thursday was classic. The laundry van would pull up and offload all the clean boilersuits, towels, and the like. The dirty Dickies being returned for cleaning along with quite a lot of unused and precious rolls of metal from the stores.

Douggie was the first entrepreneur I had ever met. He suggested we show some initiative. So, we took our own unused rolls of phosphorous to the nearby scrap metal dealer. Every night we would waddle out of the factory, hands in our pockets, past the security officers and clutching a roll of precious metal. Let's face it, they weren't at all interested in our little initiative. They were into the weekly laundry scam. I don't believe we were the only guys from the factory doing this

as the scrappies were always very pleased to see us. It only took two weeks, and I was able to stomp up the £15 to buy my first set of wheels.

It was a Friday night around 5.30pm when we turned up at the car dealers. It was not very glamorous. It was on an old war time bomb site next door to the Gosport War Memorial hospital. It was raining and not very nice. Even though he was only thirteen, I took my brother along for support. The family house in Gosport was the first house Mum and Dad had bought. It was on a large estate that was still being built. When it came to driving, I had been learning. At night when the builders had all gone home, we used to be able to go crank a handle and to start the keyless dumper trucks and drive them around the building site. This experience along with my driving my dad's company car, a Hillman Minx, through the back of the garage wall meant I wasn't a complete beginner. I already had experience of both driving and crashing.

It didn't take long to count to three, pay the man the £15 and be on our way. I'm not entirely sure how we ever got back. It was a dark rush hour in Gosport and still raining. Kangaroo hopping meant you either stalled the engine or you got lucky and made it into second gear. Then, since it was raining, there was the problem of the windscreen wipers. There was a lot to learn and quickly. I didn't know that when you put your foot on the accelerator the car would go faster, and the windscreen wipers would go slower or even stop completely. The next challenge was the steering! On a dumper truck it's very positive. On an old Ford Poplar it wasn't, and so we zig-zagged all over the road. We bumped off the kerb and because of the soppy windscreen wipers, couldn't see a bloody thing.

These were the building blocks of growing up and as beginners, we got there in the end. Having dropped brother John home with no damage done, I finally made it back to my shared digs. As time went on, and with practice, the driving thing gradually got better. Soon I was like Carlos Fandango, the legendary South American race driver. My specialty became cornering on two wheels.

Meanwhile, back at the factory, they must have found out that we were using too many rolls of expensive metals and fired a whole lot of us. This then hastened the end of my early road racing career.

Carlos Fandango

Whilst the old bill was being very busy trying to find out where all the silver phosphorus had gone, things had moved on. My dad, who was very good at his job, had been head hunted by a company called ALCOA. To make this work my parents had moved to Northfleet in Kent. This was very close to Brands Hatch racetrack and that's where my brother and I got hooked on car racing. Taking my first car to pay to pay them all a visit was an experience. I had never driven that far, and it was a long, long way.

Life was simpler as well as different back then. You got a map and followed the lines. Go to Portsmouth, go up the A3 until you bump into the South Circular road. Turn right and go all the way until the A2 when you turned right towards Dover. After twenty more miles you got to a place called Gravesend. This was where they had decided to build the next motorway, the M2. The Ford Poplar only had three gears and the approach to Gravesend was down a very long hill for three miles.

This was a new experience for me and my namesake Carlos Fandango. As we crested the hill the old A2 magically became the new M2 motorway and drag strip. The sit up and beg Ford was saying 85mph on the speedo. I've already mentioned the steering was not very precise and it took all three miles and all three lanes of the M2 to establish this new land speed record for a 1958 Ford Poplar. It was in many ways like a fairground ride with the car doing the screaming and not the passengers. As the old girl bounced around with the wings flapping and ten years of dust, doughnut bags and Coca Cola tins flying around inside the cockpit, I clung on for dear life. I realised later that I was probably very lucky to have survived this one.

Carlos Fandango and the mighty three speed Ford Poplar finally came to an end around the back of Gosport high street. One afternoon I was trying to refine the two-wheel cornering trick. Like the plonker that I was, the car went into the bend too fast and then just turned over onto its side. It was no big deal given that it only cost a few rolls of scrap metal. There was a little too much attention at the scene and there was an outstanding issue surrounding my driving license. It wasn't far from home and given all the commotion I decided to get rid of the problem by hopping on the bus.

Over the next few years there were so many cars, vans, and a motorbike. Some just didn't make it! There was the van with sliding doors that crashed upside down into the public toilets in Newham one Sunday morning. The first company car that didn't quite make the turn in the snow and crashed into the wall at the end of the road we lived in. The second company car that crashed all the way down the side of the oncoming sightseeing coach. The Cortina that caught fire going down Amersham Hill. Me and my first motorbike that were wiped out by a campervan, coming home from work one lunchtime.

Then there was the Seldram Supplies - Morris Marina, that strangely and mysteriously caught fire outside the farmhouse kitchen when I was having breakfast. The very annoying little bloke in the Ford Fiesta who really pissed me off and then couldn't stop in time. He wrecked his car on my Mercedes back bumper (ha ha). It just exploded into tiny little plastic bits like an Airfix model.

At eighteen my little brother took and passed his driving test. Being the older brother at twenty-one I felt the need to respond. With Gail's encouragement and nursing a broken arm, I too took and passed my driving test. Now my life was turning around. I was respectable as well as road legal and so we got married.

In 1971 I was married, and we went home to visit my parents, now living at Great Totham in Essex. This is of course where they make Tiptree Jam and Marmalade for the hoy-ploy, Kings and Queens as well as the rich and famous. Dad was well respected and doing good things with his work. Mum had a bicycle and was now the village post lady. Jason our old and daft dog was always still running away as well as putting it about. Brother John had borrowed some money and proudly bought his first car, not just any car but an Italian Tonka type car, with a difference.

It was a souped-up Fiat 500. It had a sunroof, bucket seats, a tiny go-faster steering wheel and sticky out wheels. We had both come down for breakfast in our pyjamas when he says, "Hey, bro, do you want to come out in me new wheels?" Being polite as well as little bit curious I said, "Yeah, man."

He's very keen to show me all the features of Fred the Fiat. We get into this giant lawnmower of a car and open the slide back bit of material that is the sunroof. Next thing you know is we're hurtling down the Essex country roads and John, all hunched up over the little rubber steering wheel, is bigging up the way it goes around corners.

It has a crude 1960s Italian version of a cruise control. You pulled a mechanical lever, which gripped the throttle cable, thereby maintaining your speed. By using this and while steering with your feet, you could sit on the back of the two seats going along with your head and half your body sticking out of the roof. It's very funny but not on our maiden voyage. It was just too cold.

There's a lot to learn when you first pass your driving test. We came racing into a bend where the farmer had just dropped a load of mud onto a wet road. Fred Fiat, John and I skidded off the road, up the side of the hedge and landed in the ditch. The farmer, who also hadn't yet had his breakfast, sat still on his tractor chewing on a blade of grass.

What he saw were two young nincompoops in what now looked like an upside down, fairground dodgem car with wide, sticky out wheels. They had come skidding sideways around *his* bend, bounced off *his* hedge, and were now lying upside down in *his* ditch. Strangely, he thought, they were still wearing pyjamas and were crawling out through the sunroof. He was expressionless, still chewing on his blade of grass and said, "Y'all right then. Suppose you want me to pull you out?"

Dad wasn't impressed though fortunately the damage was very slight. The hedge cushioned the impact which then really just left a bent bumper, some small dents on the car and a big dent in John's pride.

We had only been married a few weeks and being a Mardle was all still quite new.

Gail wasn't sure whether to be annoyed or just unimpressed.

Off to the Spa

Once married, I gradually got the idea that things had to change. Seriously, I really do think I could have been a racing driver and would have been good at it. It turned out never to be. Instead, I just had to make do with being married and helping manage Phil Dowsett Racing. My brother John was the talent, who along with his box of spanners, did all the car prep work in his garage at Malden in Essex. Along with my friend and neighbour, Rob Cavell, we found us a local team sponsor with a private aeroplane. We drove the van and added a bit of glamour to each event. However, as is life, I now had to be both responsible and serious. I always worked hard and most importantly, by 1978, was working for myself and my new family. The success of our business created opportunities that I would otherwise never have had.

In 2005 I needed a commuting car to get me from Camberley, where we lived, to Oxford each day. I couldn't really go to work in a Rolls Royce as it's not good for your company's image let alone the wear and tear cost. The dealer who supplied our vans gave me a great deal on a Renault Megane Sport which I could then use as a day by day run around. The moment you saw it, you knew it was bang on. I was taking a long time to grow up

and this car was a boy racer's dream. It sat low to the ground on fat, wide low-profile tyres on wheels that stuck out. Inside were wraparound bucket seats, a stubby little gear shift and a steering wheel that said Competition. It was a small car with a 220hp powerhouse, which was a lot of grunt for its size and weight. The brakes were fantastic, the car was perfectly balanced and went wherever you pointed it, just like a go kart.

In 2000, having survived the big Millennium meltdown! I was kindly invited by a Goodwood Road Racing Club member to attend their annual revival event. We both went to the race meeting in a beautiful old 1950s Jaguar XK120 race car, which was seriously good. Looking down the long, leather strapped bonnet it roared and bounced through all the back roads of Sussex on what is still one of my favourite road journeys. After that I was hooked, and Goodwood right from the start felt like my spiritual home. The racing history, the actual racetrack, the atmosphere, and the excitement it created in me every time I went there.

Goodwood do everything well and have a member's clubhouse, hotel and trackside venues. It was so good that I immediately joined the Goodwood Road Racing Club. The club ran some track days where you could safely (like a lunatic) drive your own car around the racetrack of champions. They put on fabulous Christmas balls, summer parties and breakfast club meetings each month. They have two race meetings a year and for a few years it had energy, was exclusive, and great fun.

In 1970 I had hitchhiked to Spa for the very last Grand Prix on the full nine-mile circuit. It was won at an average lap speed of 150mph, by a British BRM, controversially sponsored by a condom manufacturer, and driven by a Mexican, Pedro

Rodriguez. Thirty-eight years on and in 2008 the club had exclusively booked one of the best old racetracks in the world. The entire Formula One Grand Prix circuit, at Spa in Belgium, was ours on which to behave badly. It was a four-day safari with members driving their own cars all the way to a lovely Belgian hotel in the Ardennes forest. Some old and very famous racing drivers accompanied the trip. Members brought Lightweight E-Type Jaguars, GT3 Porsches, Aston Martins, as well as a selection of Ferraris and other exotic machines. We of course took Reggie the Renault!

Oh, and how we do love to dress up like in Downton Abbey. Over black tie and pre-dinner drinks people would ask you, which of your cars had you brought on this trip, and which one will you be driving? It's all a bit snotty of course. It doesn't occur to some people that not everyone has a stable of both cars as well as horses. I've become used to people bigging themselves up and it doesn't bother me anymore. After all, we were all petrol heads, here for a little drive around the countryside. For me, this is my choice and I'm going to get the most out of it. I'm happy and it's now showtime, so you go for it and always flat out.

By now the Rolly Poly had made way for the spaghetti monster. The very thought of using my precious and very expensive Ferrari 550 Maranello wasn't a good idea. Destroying a £1,300 set of Pirelli P7 tyres whilst trying not to re-model the metal Armco metal barriers was too much for me. It had taken a long time as well as a Lotus Elan, a couple of BMWs, a few Mercedes, a Rolls Royce, a Bentley and four Porsches, to get to owning a boys own Ferrari. I wasn't going to throw the Italian stallion away just because it's Spa, and that I fancied myself and was trying too hard. Anyways, it's a lot more fun in an affordable Renault Megane Sport.

The following day it was all so exciting as we all put our cars into the Formula One covered pit garages. We had to attend a drivers briefing and there followed a slow drive around the 4.5-mile circuit. Back in its day this mighty racetrack was nine miles long, on public roads, without any protections and was very dangerous.

Its safety has improved these days and as part of our drive around briefing, we were shown some very long skid marks and the bent steel Armco crash barrier. The day before someone in a £200,000 Porsche GT3 road car, had lost their no claims bonus having had a full on whoopsie and written his car off. That wasn't going to happen to Reggie the Renault!

I had done some race training and had a track racing license. I had also undertaken the AMG Hi-Speed Performance driving course around the MIRA test track at Birmingham. The highlight of which was being driven by the legend that is Richard Attwood, twice winner of the Le Mans 24 Hours race. He drove me in this SLS AMG 600, a fire spitting and roaring beast, at 220mph around the oval banked MIRA circuit.

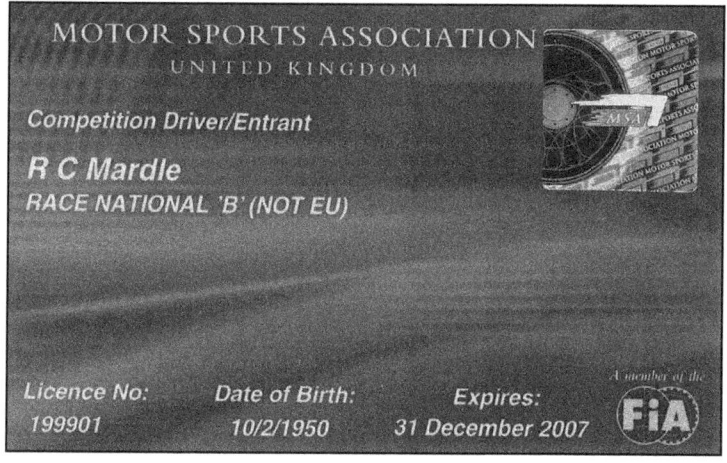

To compete at Goodwood, I had to first get a track racing license. Richard Attwood, who was also along on this trip, was the same race driver who had instructed me driving around my favourite racetrack at Goodwood. I wasn't cocky but I was now here at Spa, and I did feel confident. There comes a moment of pure magic as the green light comes on at the end of the pit road. You're now strapped in and being let out onto the legendary racetrack for the first time.

It was now Reggie the Renault vs Spa. Pedal to the metal and flat out down the long hill past the back of the pits, shifting quickly up through all six gears. Then, at

over 110mph into the legendary S-Bend that is Eau Rouge. At 210mph this bend is the ultimate adrenalin fix for a Grand Prix driver. A spectacular flat out, as fast as you can possibly go, section of bends. A little clip on the left apex, turn in and look for the second one on the right-side bend. Hold a straight line aiming for the concrete marshals post just visible over the crest of the hill. Continue to keep your foot hard to the floor for the next half mile before breaking as hard as you can for the right-left section that follows.

I had so much fun, all day long. The track is truly amazing as it rises and falls through the trees. I can't tell you how much pleasure it gives to blow off someone in a Ferrari or an Aston Martin around this great track. Reggie and I were not just fast around all the corners, we were sensational. We passed people under braking going into the corners as well as coming out of the turns. Along some of the long straights, at 130mph we would be able to slip-stream them as they went past with their greater top speed. The fun bit was clambering all over them at the next corner. I think this was my own once in a lifetime personal Grand Prix. Something I had always wanted to do.

At lunchtime Gail was allowed to drive the circuit but in a totally separate way to me. She was, after all, a trained ballerina with a driving license. They plugged her into a 1950s D-Type Jaguar for a few hot laps with another of my heroes, the legend that is Barrie 'Whizzo' Williams. At pre dinner drinks that evening it was very funny to have so many people come up to us and to say, "Weren't you man who overtook me with that little Renault?" "Yes," I would reply.

Probably one of the best days of my life.

Once Upon a Doughnut

In 1970 meeting Gail was the best thing that ever happened to me. We were both twenty and I was just another numpty, bumming around and without any direction. By then I had already been fired from so many jobs and chucked out of so many bedsits. Usually, it was because I had no money and couldn't afford to pay the rent. I would stay up all night and just couldn't be bothered to get up for work in the morning.

It wasn't so easy finding your own way and learning to grow up and live on your own. I was never lonely but sometimes you did get a bit hungry. When things got really bad, the pay-as-you-go electric meters were always helpful. If you were careful, you could open and close the padlock in such a way that it didn't look like it had been tampered with. That helped get the bus fare to work and to go shopping for some grub.

I was happily drifting, living in West Hampstead, and working with my friend from Gosport, Richard Forte. We had both been to catering college in Portsmouth. Richard came from a hotel and catering family so that gave him a degree of privilege as well as a head start on me.

Having been asked to leave school in 1965, I was still sampling 'the menu of life' which after all said and done, wasn't that bad. I never got along with the French classes at school but did remember a few critical and very helpful phrases such as, *bonjour petit pois, mange tout* and *fromage frais*. These, along with the Queen's English, helped me hitch hike all over Europe. I had some great times in those five years sneaking into many of the Formula One Grand Prix races.

As well as becoming a Euro Traveller, I had been repatriated from Italy. I was once arrested and spent the night in jail at Gray's Thurrock (nice, cooked breakfast). Been banned from driving and arrested for shoplifting from Coats and 'Ats in Portsmouth.

The Italian hitchhike gig was good. Luigi, a mate of Dudley's, inherited his grandfather's house at Lugano somewhere in northern Italy. One evening, sitting around, we decided what a great idea to pop over there and see what it was all about. Dudley, Richard, and a few of us decided we would find our own ways there. That we would all meet up, wherever there was, in a weeks' time.

I wasn't actually doing anything much at that time having just been fired from what I thought was the best job in the world, working at *Motor Sport* the magazine. I was actually very good at the job, and I still don't know or understand how that even happened. I was enthusiastic, never late, and turned up every day to work in the advertising department. I interacted well with the clients, which on one occasion aged 18, had even led to my taking a coach full of enthusiasts to Le Mans for a weekend.

One day, I came back from lunch (shepherd's pie and a cup of tea paid for with luncheon vouchers). On the desk was a letter from the miserable big boss saying I was fired. No explanation or appeal just don't come back. This was the first job I ever wanted or liked. It's no wonder then, that for me, dossing around was far better than trying for another pointless job!

Like everything nasty that life dishes out, you get over it. It took me a week of hitchhiking and train hopping to get to Piacenza south of Milan (great railway station). I discovered at the Paris Gar-de-Sud, there was a posh old train called the Eurostar-Express that travelled from Paris to Rome. Without a ticket, and before getting on, it was strategically very important. You had to decide who and where the train manager and ticket collector were. It was a case of strategic thinking, which way along the train they were going. If they were at the front, then you got on the back and visa-versa.

They spent so much time talking nicely to the posh old customers that it took them a long time to get from the front to the back of the train. When they did finally catch up with you, it turned out they weren't very good at understanding English. I was, of course, always polite as well as playing the stupid card and so, for them it just all became too much trouble. I was on my own and so they just put me in the baggage van and threw me off at the next stop. The beauty of this strategy was that the train didn't stop very often and so you got to go a very long way.

Having missed the first meeting point at Milan station, I went on to find Lugano which wasn't so hard. What wasn't so easy was finding Luigi's new, old Italian palace. Good luck always plays a big part when you're hitchhiking around. Getting a ride, somewhere to sleep, something to eat, and so on. I ended up happily sitting in the sun, in the small village square of Lugano munching a *donut del dia*. Well, who should pop up but the boys who, they said, were also looking out for me. Truth was they were shopping having run out of cornflakes.

Luigi's newly inherited house had no electricity or running water. The Casa Italiano turned out to be a long walk from anywhere, rundown and falling apart. It was also a long way from Camden Town and so was very cool. We were taught well by our parents and so washed every day in a nearby stream which had a wooden dam. To have a shower/bath you dropped the sluice gates in and waited for the water to back up. You took your clothes off and with a bar of soap, jumped in. There was a rope to pull open the gate and then 'bosh' you all but drowned in the freezing water. Although it was summer in the middle of Italy, we must have been high up and the freezing cold stream was fed from the snow-capped mountains.

It was cold in the evenings, so we had to light a wood fire to keep warm, and slept on the floor in our sleeping bags. Dudley used to get spooked by the rats and mice which you felt running across you in your sleeping bag when you were asleep. They of course were pleased to have some company and ran around happily all night looking for the secret cornflake stash.

Like everything at the University of Life it was a wonderful experience. Eventually we got hungry and fed up with eating cornflakes. Luigi was a clever guy. He could read and write in joined-up writing. With these skills he had a decent job working as a trainee reporter for the Associated Press on Fleet Street. By now he'd used up all his compassionate time off work (the dead benevolent grandpa). So, nothing else for it and it was time to go back home. There wasn't much to pack up. We had probably burnt the front door whilst keeping warm, there were no windows to close and so we just walked away. I wonder now if, after all the years, Luigi ever went back?

The others all had the means, and I as always, had no money. It was amazing to find out that if you went to the British Consulate, they were duty bound to assist you. I told them a Jackanory about not being well. That I had been abandoned by my friends and did not have any money. So, it turned out that they had a duty to help. They provided a third-class train ticket all the way to Dover with just enough money for a daily food allowance, so I didn't have to eat any more cornflakes. The downside was that they scribbled all over my passport in red pen. This meant that the immigration man at Dover confiscated my passport. He told me that I couldn't have it back until the debt to Her Majesty's Government was repaid. No more hitchhiking for a while then.

Richard and I lived in the ground floor apartment at number two Parsifal Road, West Hampstead. Freddie and his piano lived on the top floor. Freddie Allan was a musician and a guitarist who once upon a time had been in a 1960's chart topping band called Peter and Gordan. He was still getting royalties from that time, so he didn't really need to work. He sat at his piano, wrote songs, and believed his new band, Urban Clearway, were going to be very successful. While getting established they needed a van to carry their gear around to gigs, which wasn't very often. So, in the daytime we all sort of worked together as Forte and Allan Transport.

I was newly out of work and homeless once again. Richard was really good at looking out for me offering me somewhere to live and a job of sorts. It was the nineteen sixties and more fun hanging out and working for these two guys. I wasn't ready to try and make myself wake up every day and to do some awful job that I really didn't like. I didn't get paid, but I did get somewhere to sleep, food and the odd £10 when it was needed.

Now, F-A Transport had two useful vans and, from somewhere? a three-wheel BMW bubble car which we must somewhere down the way, have been asked to dispose of. We reckoned that because of its size and ability to go up and down alleys, it was probably used in a jewellery robbery or something similar. It needed to get lost, and we were stupid enough to help out.

It was surprisingly quick, noisy. The way in and out was the whole of the front of this contraption. When you pulled the wire door handle the whole front, windscreen steering wheel and bodywork, opened outwards and upwards. We were young, brave, and very thin in those days. Somehow, you could actually get the three of us, sitting side by side, on the one and only seat. It was like a giant motorised fishbowl using a large, moped engine. It was super noisy, and we

would charge down the busy Finchley Road, the road only inches away from our bums. You changed gears using a gear shift that was like a super strong indicator stalk located under the steering wheel.

Going out in this thing, we would always get the giggles. It was so normal to hit the bends and for it to tip up in the air onto two wheels. Us giggling idiots in the car had to lean over really quickly to rebalance the flying bubble and to get the wheel back on the ground. Despite our best efforts we never turned it over. It certainly wasn't very practical. There was nowhere to put the shopping or Fred's guitar. I don't remember how and when we got rid of it. Most likely it just ran out of petrol and so we had probably got out and just left it.

We worked for just about anyone and for an hourly rate of £1/10 shillings. We were sort of like three male prostitutes, anytime, anywhere, and anything goes. In 1969 we had a good summer thanks to the dustman's strike. The posh people of Chelsea and Knightsbridge wanted their stinky rubbish taken away. We just went round collecting more and more of the black bags charging a pound a bag and no questions asked. It was a hot summer so by the end of the day, with a full van load, it used to get really hard to breathe. We would seek aspirational relief by taking them all to the Chelsea rubbish tip at Lotts Road. Still, someone had to do it and it made good money.

The green van, which was our one, had sliding doors for the driver and passenger. In those ignorant days, seat belts weren't legally required, and so nobody wore them. Our day usually  kicked off by driving down to the Kings Road in Chelsea, doors open, feet sticking out the sides and pirate radio stations blasting out loud. The Chelsea bakehouse sold a bag full of hot, just baked jam doughnuts for £1. We always ended up so sticky but totally made up for the day.

We worked regularly for C P Burge, the very posh Sloane Street Antique dealer. Our time was spent lugging very expensive pieces to the workshops and to his clients. Mr Burge's workshops were at Kingston on Thames. It was there that they would make 'antique' furniture, tables, chairs, wooden picture frames and mirrors and the like. Then they would 'antique it' by using hammers, crow bars, chains, and lots of the make-it-look-and-smell-old, PT Wax. All very genuine – not!

We also did all the deliveries for Abruzzi's high-end and very trendy, modern plastic furniture. We were given our delivery instructions and then had to go dig it all out of the Harrods Depository down on the riverfront at Fulham. It's still there but these days it's now a block of trendy upmarket riverside flats overlooking the river Thames. The people at Harrods couldn't count and nor could we. We often ended up with an inconvenient piece of left over furniture which we then had to sell off to pay for more of the doughnuts.

Our nicest clients were Mr and Mrs Dennis De Jersey Jones. They were posh, upmarket, interior designers, and estate agents. As well as our helping out with the property business, our job seemed to be assisting in people's extra marital affairs. One day we would be moving bedroom furniture, lamps and rugs into a luxury apartment that Dennis had for sale. The next day we would be moving it all out again. The De J-Js were a lovely, glamorous couple. They were very well connected and working for them we got to meet some very famous people. As a property agent Dennis was a great one for spotting a deal. He would buy antique furniture from old country houses. We would go collect it for him to sell onto his newest clients to furnish their newly acquired London apartments.

We did the lugging and shoving, and the tips were good! The nicest thing I can remember was that they liked us, and they often fed us in their lovely Chelsea apartment. They referred to us as 'the Boys'. It was all so like being in one of those old TV shows that they hadn't yet thought of or made. *Minder* or an upmarket *Only Fools and Horses*. Dennis was the posh, real deal version of Del Boy and we were like a right pair of Rodneys.

All this, of course, was exhausting! Most days we would stop off (after the doughnuts) and have coffee and toast in a coffee shop off Baker Street. It was here that I met Gail who had dropped out of the Arts Educational School for budding ballerinas because of illness. She was probably still in recovery, drifting around, waiting for prince charming to rock up with a snazzy car and a Coutts private bank account. She was helping her friend Hillary, whose father owned the film company upstairs and this ground floor coffee bar. There was Gail, Hillary and four other girls all living together in their George Street flat just around the corner from Selfridges in Oxford Street.

It was central London in 1970 and somehow this was just the way things were. She smoked long, very expensive looking, Dunhill cigarettes and ironed her hair every day. She wore very short 'hot pants', stick-on false eyelashes, and platform shoes. It was all a bit bonkers in those days. People wore wide kipper ties, flared trousers and three-inch-tall platform shoes and boots. We all looked forward to the top ten selling pop records played at 6pm on Sundays, every week. We had groundbreaking pirate radio stations and dark, moody night-time discotheques. London was a really cool place to live and to be a part of. It

also had the Playboy Club in Park Lane where my flash mate Richard was of course a member.

Now, being a member gave you and a guest free admission so you could drink and if you had any money, gamble. Being young and up for fun we always got along with the girls who worked dressed up as rabbits. We never had any money, so gambling wasn't an option. There was always a free buffet so we could top up on our doughnut and toast diet, by dining out regularly at our Park Lane, London club.

Lawrence of Arabia

Gail and I went out on our first date. I asked her if she wanted to go to see the big movie of the day, *Lawrence of Arabia*, on at the Odeon Kensington High Street. I can understand why she was playing hard to get, when she reluctantly agreed to meet me there. I think I suggested we meet inside, so that I didn't have to pay for her! To be fair it wasn't because I was mean, it was just I didn't have much money.

It was helpful then that Gail didn't like popcorn or ice creams. Thank goodness we liked the film, and that left us getting along just fine. Although it wasn't part of a plan, she still didn't ask me to her upcoming twenty-first birthday party.

No matter, as they say, you snooze you lose. To tidy myself up, I needed to have a shave, a bath and to wash my hair. To borrow a shirt from Freddie, a pair of boots from Richard and a Bedford van from Dennis De Jersey Jones. I thought it would be a lovely surprise and impress her by gate-crashing the party at the family home at Penn in Berkshire. In those days there was no motorway and so you tanked it down the A40 dual carriageway, which ran out west to the rich and affluent home counties.

In the back of the borrowed work van, was an antique King George III dining room table worth thousands of pounds. Two wheeled cornering was a technique I had mastered years ago in my first (RIP) car. The King's table started moving around a lot with each and every roundabout, and there were lots of those. By the time I got to Manor Road, where Gail's family lived, I had discovered, for the very first time, they had speed bumps. We never had those in London as the traffic never went fast enough. This was clearly an idea by provincial rich people to slow down robbers who were trying to get away from the house they had just robbed. It gave the old plod a bit longer to race to the scene of the crime and arrest the blaggards.

Fortunately, unlike Habitat and Ikea, furniture was tough in those days! King George, who had been dead for a long, long time, wouldn't get to find out about his table, which had probably never been out of London. Good old PT-Wax always fixed most things.

I know we hadn't known each other for very long. Gail, who was probably still playing the hard-to-get card, gave the impression of being very cross with me for just turning up. Her friends and invited guests were standing around sipping gin and tonics and going, yah, yah, yah. I didn't know anyone or had ever had a gin and tonic. I was always up for fun and so launched myself into the party which went on until very late. I had a really fun time and I certainly got everyone going.

I slept on the settee that night and met my mother-in-law-to-be, the following day. I was brought up to be polite and confident. She didn't feel threatened by me and so was also nice and charming. Little did she, or us, know what was to come of all this. Gail needed to get back to George Street and so accepted the lift back to London in 'the van'. I don't think that she had ever been in one before. We celebrated her birthday back at the shared flat in James Street and 'bingo', before we knew it, we were a couple. At that time, I didn't have a pot to pee in. I made her laugh and was unpredictable and always on the lookout for fun.

My first driving career as well as working for myself came to an end one unfortunate weekend. I took on a special mission for a Mr Costa-Hempel. He was either very rich on antique furniture or drugs and I didn't care which. He was cool and so was his lovely Russian wife, Anoushka.

He wanted me to drive and pick up somewhere between London and the English Channel in Kent. I needed some muscle. We were to collect some really heavy and very old furniture from some old castle or something. I asked my friend Dudley to come along for the ride.

He'd never been out of London and had never seen real live cows, sheep, and stuff. Lots of young, working people, living in London, had never been out into the country. I was OK with that as my dad had driven us all over the south of England in the course of his work. I knew what a cow looked like! With a bag full of leftover doughnuts, we set off really early, well at 8am one Sunday morning. We used the AA handbook as it was free, and every driver had one. It included maps and told us which roads to use and where to stop for a pee and tea.

It was still mid-winter and cold. The roads down through South London were wet and it was very smoggy/foggy. I'm not entirely sure what sort of roll ups Dudley was smoking but being so cold, we kept the doors and windows closed with the heater on. The Commer van had sliding doors and like the BMW bubble car, a column gear shift and three gears. Radio Caroline was our preferred pirate radio station. We were very happy trolling along smoking and eating doughnuts while still waking up after a late Saturday night. No one drank alcohol in those days, but we did like to hang out talking, playing records, and laughing until very late.

The fog got thicker and the visibility in Clapham, Balham and Crasham got seriously bad. We came down the hill to New Cross, a graveyard and accident black spot according to the AA map. I was struggling to see through the foggy gloom and the smoke from Dudley's roll ups. Suddenly a set of unseen traffic lights ran out into the road. Oh, bugger, I thought. I was hoping to take my driving test some day and I knew if traffic lights were Red, that means you had to stop.

Even though we had set off at the crack of dawn, instinct and my lightning-fast reactions took over. I can clearly remember to this day how we did the Hokey Cokey, swerving first to the left and then moving to the right. The van with no load in, was very light and no

thoroughbred sports car that's for sure. It didn't cope very well with the Hokey Cokey and so, with a mind of its own, just gave up and turned over. It slid across the road avoiding the pigeons and oncoming traffic. It was amazing not to have hit anything until it came crashing into the magnificent Victorian public toilets where it then stopped.

Dudley and I found ourselves in the back of the van, along with Radio Caroline's Tony Blackburn who was playing a favourite Beatles song of the time, 'Help'. The back doors had come open, and the van was just lying there, on its back, waving its legs in the air with a huge cloud of smoke coming from the inside. The few Sunday morning passers-by thought it was probably on fire and ran away. It wasn't of course, well not yet. It was only Dud's bloody aromatic roll ups. We both agreed to leave the AA book and just to leg it before anyone came along and started asking awkward questions.

Like I said, it was very smoggy/foggy both outside and inside the van. Smog was a widespread problem of the 1960s and a result of industry and everyone burning coal. A law banning coal was now in place but was still taking a while to have an effect. The worst case was when smog combined with fog and the visibility came down to ten or twenty feet.

With so very few people around no one seemed to notice us. We decide to go hide away in a nearby café, get a cup of strong tea, with lots of sugar and we could watch, wait, and see. It was really funny sitting there amongst the few regulars who, on a smoggy Sunday morning, were hungover, very excited and discussing this unusual turn of events.

The Northern line runs slowly on Sunday mornings, and we took until lunchtime to get back to our cave. The hospital plastered my broken arm and put it in a sling. Dudley, once I had explained to him what had happened, was all OK and very relaxed about the whole episode.

It's a funny old world. Our mentor, Dennis De Jersey Jones,

was so very cool about the whole thing. It's not often that someone steals his van and heads for the channel ports on a Sunday morning. He had the insurers collect the baby Commer which was quickly put back on its feet then, despite the big drama, easily fixed. The funny thing was when we got it back, it always smelled of toilet blocks and pee.

We did a couple more jobs for Costa and D-D-J-J before retiring from the transport business. Gail, by now my sleeping partner, had decided what I was doing was dangerous and probably illegal. She made me get a proper job and move into a one room bedsit in Balcombe Street. I knew **she wasn't very impressed**, and I still don't think she was very convinced about me at that point. I was, however, still just an interesting and randy bit of rough with no fancy set of wheels, no private bank, and no future.

Avoiding Public Lavatories

After the van wrecking show in Newham in 1970, my life started to take a whole new direction. I did discover that, for a few years, I couldn't bring myself to use a public toilet!

We were getting very good at sleeping together, up close, and very personal, in a single bed in our very cosy little Balcombe Street room. There was a big cupboard in the corner, by the window. You opened the door and inside there, discreetly hidden away, was a tiny little cooker and a sink. The 'apartment' came with a small table and two hard chairs by the window. It was around this time, without a fridge to look after the food, milk and stuff, that we started to drink black coffee and eating lots of cereals. The whole room was probably 12ft x 12ft. It was bright, clean and somehow it just worked. The toilet and shower cubicle were a share and halfway down the staircase. To have a shower you had to put a shilling in the meter and, for what is now five pence, not take too long! Living in bedsits is a whole way of life and thousands of us did it. You got very used to co-existing alongside your neighbours and to be fair, rarely ever saw them.

Balcombe Street was a nice street just of Baker Street, in a decent neighbourhood. The Irish Republican Army thought so as well and for a while they become my neighbours. This didn't go down well with Gail or the Metropolitan Police. For a whole week the IRA threatened to blow up our little love nest, as well as the rest of the street. So, for a while we had to move out.

Gail had by now found me a proper job and so now we both had normal jobs, off we went to work every day. That meant getting up at the same time and not being late for work. The 'jobs' gave us both these bits of printed paper called luncheon vouchers as part of our twenty pounds a week pay. This was quite normal back in the early seventies, and the luncheon vouchers themselves tasted awful, worse than cornflakes. We were, after all, both new to all this 'going to work and being normal' stuff. Someone a lot more mature than us, had to explain they weren't necessarily for eating at lunchtimes, as the name suggested. That they should and could be exchanged for food in cheap restaurants and cafes. I suppose this was one step up from Red Cross parcels or the food coupons we used to have after the war.

These were good then since it meant you could go out and spend them in the evenings, in nice proper places. Gail and I used to go to eat at the really cool, just arrived from the USA, American style 'Tennessee Pancake House'. It was located at the top of Baker Street and very easy to get to on the number twenty-four bus. Remember this was 1970 and just before the 2nd great plague, that is McDonalds and Burger King, had been invented. You had real shiny cutlery and proper plates. The LVs didn't go that far but we were both hooked on their cheesy pancakes. When we didn't have enough to pay the bill it was really quite easy. Having finished all your food, you watched carefully and waited for the twenty-four bus to Victoria, to pull up outside. At the very last minute we just got up quickly, legged it out the double doors, and giggling like the pair of muppets we were, jumped onto the open platform at the back of the bus as it pulled away. People were always jumping on and off the back of the buses and so no-one ever paid it any attention.

My younger brother, at eighteen went and passed his driving test getting a proper full driving license. I was by then twenty-one and this wasn't on. So, in trying to gain some respectability Gail said I should have a go. After all it couldn't be that hard, loads of other people, including my baby brother, had one! By this time the driving ban on my provisional license, which of course, was all a terrible misunderstanding, had run out. And the license had now been returned to me.

I needed to take a few driving lessons since I had acquired a few rude habits while driving the vans. I would pull up at the driving school, in the newly repaired Commer van and my broken arm in a sling. The instructor would throw a hissy fit, calm down and off we would go and complete the lesson. On the big day, I did a lot of waving my arms out of the window and I spent more time looking in the rear-view mirror than looking forwards at the road. Luckily the hand signals bit involved my right arm and not the injured left one! I passed the driving test and now I was right-proper, legal, and allowed to join in the road chaos officially.

I kept in touch with my good friends and for a while was roadie for Freddy, the dreamer, and his band, Urban Clearway.

They mostly played hot and smoky pubs and every now and then a bigger gig. One of those was at a huge London college. Elton John and his band were just making the pop headlines and they were the main act. We rocked up in our slightly used, old, Ford Transit van and parked next to the big, pink, star-studded bus. We were the support band and looked like the poor relations. Gail and her friend Anthea came along and sat posing on the stage smoking long Dunhill menthol cigarettes. We did our set. Then the main man with his really weird, don't talk to us we're really so important, band kicked off. Reggie, who was by this time now called Elton, leaned over and spoke to Gail. The huge star-to-be said these words which of course they will never forget, "Get off my stage." Well now, what could they say. It's OK because I had already met the great and little man. He had already told me to not to look at him or to stand behind him in the wings. WOW, to now think we had gigged, and both had conversations with Reg Dwight, the tubby little rock legend and megastar that is now Elton John.

As much as I might have liked the way things were, there comes a time when the game's up. Gail had decided I had to grow up and to get a proper job and so, who was I to argue? The trouble with all this respectability was that it didn't pay enough, and I was suffering from bad doughnut withdrawal symptoms'. Twenty pounds a week and a packet of food vouchers. No sense complaining so I had to go and get another job.

So, I went and got a job working Saturdays at Dormy Menswear in Soho. I had to camp it up a bit and learn to mince and talk differently. The boss told me it was important to tell people how good they looked in their hire suits and hats. It's funny how easily I took to selling the add-ons like the cufflinks and ties. Maybe, if I did but know it, this was a sign of the future?

While all this was going on, we delighted ourselves by deciding we needed a bigger bed, and so we got married in November 2021. My 'in-laws-to-be' were not best pleased or happy about it. With good reason they thought I was a waste of space, which by and large was true. When doing their due diligence, they found out that my mum had been a school dinner lady and was now the village post lady for Great Totham, the home of Tiptree jams and marmalades. That I had been expelled from both school and the catering college. I had no GCSEs, an impounded passport, and there was some confusion regarding the status of my driving license.

Gail who, in deciding to marry me, had finally come round to my way of thinking. By now I had a job at Butlin's holiday camps head office, a full driving license and a way of making her laugh and be happy. Strange then that there was a bit if family resistance to the idea of our getting married. On that point Gail stood her ground and so my mother-in-law-to-be, bought Gail an engagement ring for ten pounds.

My father-in-law-to-be, Jim, was a gambling man and I think he liked the odds. In his world daughters were not so important as sons. However, and to his great credit, he quietly supported us. He gave us a superb big wedding in a very posh hotel, the Complete Angler at Marlow. Talk about being out of my depth. That was a glamorous but very odd occasion. It was a bit like West Ham playing Wycombe Wanderers in the FA Cup. With so many of my Rizla packing roll up cousins, uncles and aunties, rubbing shoulders with the cigar smoking 'hoi polloi' of

High Wycombe. On a good note, Moss Bros did very well that week. It made for a very interesting mix. Because of my Saturday job, I got a very good deal on the fancy dress costumes, for best man Richard, and my brother.

Gail's father and his friends had such a lot to do with making the post-war town of High Wycombe what it then was. They started the cricket and rugby clubs, the Round Table and Chamber of Commerce. Jim was responsible for helping rebuild the town centre around his four-floor department store named Murrays, after his father. This made Jim the sheriff, and his cigar smoking, champagne guzzling mates, the deputies.

It wasn't too hard to spot my uncles, aunties, friends, and cousins. They were the ones drinking the beer and smoking a lot of roll ups. My mum still had a bag on and was barely talking to me. I do hope they felt some pride and pleasure at our wedding and maybe where Gail and I might be going. I am and always will be, very grateful to Jim for bringing both our families together and giving us a chance. The odds were long, and I hope he came out on top with the bookies.

My dad paid for us to go on a honeymoon to Majorca. I had never been on an aeroplane before. To get my passport back we had to repay the government for my food packet and the get you home, Italian train ticket. I'm sure I would have told her eventually and travelling to Majorca wasn't possible without this very important document! Not for the first time,
Gail wasn't very impressed.

My mother-in-law was always outspoken and had a lot to say about Gail marrying such a no hoper as me. This was a bit rich considering, as it turned out, that her first marriage was to a bus conductor! Right from the beginning she took up a position and that has lasted some fifty-plus years. She clearly told me, the day before we went to the wedding factory, that I wasn't good enough. She told me she was against the wedding and that Gail should be marrying a prince or something like that. She wasn't wrong of course but given the right encouragement, people and things can change.

They had tried to buy Gail off and get her to walk away with money and a go-anywhere-in-the-world ticket. Jim, however, being the man that he was, kept his head down and helped us right from the start. His company, Murrays, had a two-bedroomed part-furnished empty flat in Beaconsfield. For a token rent paid to the company, we could use it to help get ourselves going. There were no curtains and no heating, it was December, and it was freezing. So, as we huddled around the gas cooker in the kitchen, we started a new chapter in both our lives.

From being carefree, how quickly things had changed. We both started commuting using the train to London, Marylebone. From the station to Butlin's head office on Oxford Street, I had to catch the same number twenty-four bus we used to use as a getaway vehicle when ripping off the Tennessee pancake house restaurant.

Gail's brother, Richard, had returned from working in South Africa. It turned out that we had plenty in common and hit if off immediately. We both liked his sister. We had both been on an aeroplane. We both had full driving licenses and importantly, a job. Richard, along with his girlfriend Yvonne (who was evidently so inspired by us, that she later became his wife), moved into the ice palace with us. This was of course very helpful. Even though the bathroom was a life changing daily challenge, we could now afford to light the little gas fire in the sitting room as well as the kitchen.

Gail still wasn't sure.

Flying a Car

It always takes me a while to work things out, and then one day, it dawned on me. That like other people instead of paying rent, we could probably get and pay for a mortgage. Father-in-law Jim and I seemed to be getting along very well. With his patient help, he had taught me to drink whisky without choking and spluttering. It seemed that whenever you went to the house, whatever time of day it was, you had to have a whisky with him. This was OK by me and so after a quick snifter, I put the idea of a mortgage to him. He was always a man of few words and he said, "Good idea."

Once the driving license misunderstanding had been cleared up, he kept insisting I drove his lovely Jaguar XJ6 car. This was very brave as we didn't have a car and to be fair, I did have some sort of track record! This was one of the best cars of its day. Leather seats, reputation, automatic and powerful. I was twenty-one and, once in his Jag, felt and behaved like I was the mutt's nuts. I was young, stupid, and fitted in with all the other 'well to do idiots' from Beaconsfield. Mother-in-law Joan would, when necessary, lend me her 'Sunbeam Sport Fastback' car to go about house hunting.

Back in the seventies it was a case of taking a bog-standard

car from the factory. Sticking on a rev counter, a funky steering wheel, some plastic wheel trims and a pair of bucket seats. Then put a badge on the boot that said GLX Sport, add a picture of Jackie Stewart, world champion, and hey presto! a thousand pounds added to the price. For an idiot like me this was so like the car that Bill McGovern drove at Brands Hatch every week.

The further you go away from London, the lower the house prices. We both had jobs in London and of course, didn't want to live in Yorkshire. The search area that we could afford produced some very interesting choices. I found us a fabulous little two-bedroomed, sixteenth century house, in the centre of a little Hertfordshire village called Aldbury. The nearby town was Tring where, quite by chance, Gail had gone to ballet school for six years. We agreed a price of £7,250 and we were over the moon and extremely excited. I raced back in the little white Fastback Sunbeam, GLSX Sport, to tell Gail.

There's a little hump-back bridge on the road out of the village. You're not allowed to call them "hump backed" anymore. Instead, they are probably now referred to as "inverted jelly mould bridges". When I wasn't pretending to be a Grand Prix driver, I would be a champion rally driver. I was heading for the main road and concentrating on the rev counter while the hedges were whizzing by. At the last minute, looking up in horror, I spotted the upcoming bridge. Suddenly all four wheels of the car left the ground, and we were flying. The problem of course was obvious in that cars don't fly, and even GLSX Sport road cars are definitely not built to leave the ground. This unscheduled flight then came down with a terrible crash.

As the driver I was supposed to be in control. For a moment I was having quite a struggle avoiding the hedges, the wall, the ditch and probably all the wildlife who still lived there. Your subconscious registered the experience, gathered everything up and carried on back to base all the wiser and ready for perhaps the next time.

What I didn't know was that when the flight was over, and the car hit the ground, all the oil had escaped from the bottom of the engine. Gail's dear old uncle Digby was a great help in clearing up the mess and repairing the car. M-in-law, of course, wasn't amused. Once again it just confirmed how right she had been about me all along. I don't remember Jim ever lending me his Jaguar after that.

By now I was doing quite well in the growing up department and we had learned how to be married, got our first mortgage and were commuting each day, to work in London. The gorgeous little house was small and lovely but a bit chilly. So, we went and bought double glazed windows and night storage heating from Everest who kept telling us they were the best. They were bought on what they called 'the drip'. This meant they got paid for, each week, in little amounts, over a few years.

Once again, my whole world had changed. In the space of two years, I had gone from being unemployed, single, and living in a bedsit, to being married, with a mortgage, central heating and living in a little country village.

Having night storage heaters was a blessing and a curse. At night, inside these great big heavy heater boxes were hundreds of little electricians. They ran around really, really fast all night long getting very hot in the process. They then hid all this heat they made, in special little bricks. Come daytime, and before they went to bed, they opened the heaters flaps a little bit so as too slowly let out all the heat they had made and stored. On a really cold day you woke up and it was lovely and warm. On a hot sunny day, it was crazy. You couldn't reason with these guys who in the 1970's belonged to STUFF, the Small Trade Union of Freethinking Firelighters. It's ironic that 50 years on nothing has changed! For us, that meant we had a bit of an energy crisis and so I had to find a part-time job so we could pay the bills.

Living out in the country, we needed a car to get to the station and anywhere else for that matter. We purchased a 1958 Morris Minor for £95. It was too old to have a rev counter, bucket seats or anything else funky. Believe me when I say it was incapable of taking off over the little bridge. Still, it went everywhere and served us well for a while.

I interviewed for a Friday night job in a local bakery. I told them how much I liked bread. That my love of cheese and onion rolls had got me through growing up alone, once my mother had abandoned me. They were really very nice people to work for and boy oh boy, when everyone else was asleep, they really made you work hard. Again, nothing's ever wasted. I learned a few more life skills such as how to make a bucket of bread dough into one hundred bread rolls.

It's really quite simple. You lobbed all the flour, yeast and margarine into the big old machine machine and turned it. Then to make it all stick together you chucked in a bucket of water, added a pinch of salt, and tried not to sneeze over it all. Once it was mixed up, you measured out one hundred bits of dough. Then, using both hands, roll two bread rolls at the same time. All very useful and definitely worth putting on your CV. Now with petrol at 2/6d a gallon it paid good money and I proudly got to bring home a newly baked loaf of bread, made by me.

Everyone who lived in the village was a character. Our next-door neighbours were lovely. On one side a cranky lawyer, Roger, and his wife Rosemary. He liked playing with trains and polishing his car, a 1953 MG Roadster. On the other side of us was Mary Wimbush, a hard drinking BBC personality and her posh boy barrister son. Out the back lived a successful pop singer, Labi Siffre. I suppose, and not for the first time in our married life, we just felt a bit ordinary. We were under pressure and felt a bit plain and ordinary. We had to up our game and so we bought a crazy dog called Jason, a lovely great big red setter.

We lived in a perfect place for owning a dog. From outside the house, wherever you went, you were in open countryside or walking up through the woodland and onto the ridges. Jason was as mad as a hatter and being part Irish had a mind of his own. The novelty of owning a dog quickly wore off. The worst part was coming home after work on a cold and maybe wet day and then having to take the dog out for a walk. It wasn't right to not give a big dog a decent walk and so off I would go, up the trail, into and around the woods. It would feel like you had tramped a couple of miles when you would then whistle and try and find the bloody dog who you haven't seen for five minutes. Eventually I would just give up and take twenty minutes or so to get back home. When I eventually did get there, I would find he had been home a long while and was now sleeping by our lovely and warm night storage heaters.

When we went to work in the week, we had this smart idea of running a zip line down the back of the house to the boundary. Jason could stay in the dry or freely move up and down the line all day long. He was such a cunning tart and would whimper and moan when anyone was looking. Our neighbour, Labi Siffre, was a nice guy who loved our daft dog. Without our asking, he would take him in and sing him songs and tell him stories. He ended up looking after Jason every day while we went to work.

Still trying to fit into village life I made myself some strap on bells, found some clean hankies and joined the local Aldbury Morris men. That was so much fun and through them I learned to drink beer, sing along, and listen to some great old folk music in the village barn every other week. We made some lovely and talented new friends, in particular Rod and Jenny Puddefoot, who could sing, write songs, and tell great stories. "Puddefoot", now that's a name that says it all. It's like a name from the *Lord of the Rings*, a fabulous book which I first read about this time.

Looking back some fifty years, this time and place was so the England that people of my generation remember. It was nothing particularly special, it was just how you would still want it to be. It wasn't perfect, although nothing ever is for long. For a couple of years, it was a lovely time in our lives. We had learned to cook and to have country picnics and to drink wine (Liebfraumilch). We had Habitat furniture, a bath and no shower. A tiny ten inch black and white TV with three channels and a coat hanger aerial shoved up its bottom. A record player and five or six long playing vinyl records. We hung out with our neighbours and once a fortnight looked forward to the singing and the laughter at the village ceilidh.

The Morris dancers practiced every week and, just like Elton John, we toured from time to time. We hung out with good friends from Gail's side of life, Mark and Jenny, Caroline and Martin, Chris and Jo. This was the time of *Doctor Who*, *Monty Python*. The hi-spot of the week was BBC Radio's top ten best-selling records, on every Sunday afternoon. It was presented by some over excited DJ who fifty years later would be arrested and charged with some sort of indecent offences. Everyone in the country, aged under twenty-five, listened to it. We had a village pub, post office and a garage. We also had a fifty mile an hour national speed limit and petrol rationing vouchers. I wonder, do people and places like this still exist or with all the technology, progress and cleverness, have we just destroyed that time and place and all the good things that made it all come together.

The Morris Minor had by now served its purpose. With the

money from working at the bakery all night we bought another and slightly better car from the village garage. It was a 1966 Vauxhall Viva which was immediately improved by replacing the original steering wheel with a smaller Sterling Moss version. The Morris Minor sold for £15 and drove itself to the scrap yard when it failed its MOT.

May it rest in pieces.

Och-Aye-Jimmy

I may have been chucked out of school, but not all was wasted. I could read, write and was particularly good with numbers. I could also roll two balls of dough into two bread rolls at the same time! I was doing quite well in the job that Gail had found me, working for Butlin's holiday camps. I have a lot to thank my schooling for. I may not have been the most attentive or frequent participant, but the teachers were quite tough in those days. Mr Perry, our math's teacher, had played for England. He was exceptionally good at throwing the wooden blackboard rubber at you from a distance. If you were not paying attention he would come and get his rubber back and pull you along by your ear. You were then made to sit at the front of the class, and he would pick on you throughout the rest of the lesson. The thing is, between Mr Perry and Mr Newell I somehow learned to be good at basic maths and rubbish at algorithms and algebra.

In my new job each day I correlated and prepared all the booking statistics, from across all the eight holiday camps. I did this aged twenty-one, with Telex machines sending in the data and a Mark 1 adding machine, which had just replaced the Abacus. None of your fancy computers, or calculators, they came later. Every day I would have to take handwritten and combined numbers to the company's MD, Robert Butlin. He was treated by everyone as "God". I don't believe he ever said anything to me other than "thank you".

The English teachers at school were usually ladies and they were not as good at throwing wooden missiles like the men. I was a good reader and from an early age had a love for reading books. I did not need to be prompted, in fact quite the opposite. I read good and bad books, the Beano and Eagle comics as well as all the Marvel Comics publications about super-heroes. Added to this was the simple pleasure and excitement of "just reading". I learned so much from doing it. I am quite sure this is why, sixty years on, I am still very good at spelling, and have acquired a decent vocabulary. More importantly, this all helped when it came to doing my job. As well as preparing all the statistics for our leader, I also represented the head office replying to all the customers written complaints and, when they couldn't take anymore, their early departures. So school, it turns out, is and was very important.

I was working for a man called Mr Martin Pegg. He was a great no nonsense character who smoked non-stop, Capstan full strength unfiltered cigarettes. Back in the 1970s the packet was allowed to proudly promote the power and strength you were getting for your 2/6d. The aptly named Mr Pegg only had a few front teeth, stained brown from all the fags he smoked. He didn't do chit chat and never talked about anything in general. When he wanted you, he would just shout, and you were expected to just come running. He always said it like it was, told you what he wanted and didn't tolerate fools. I liked him and I think I got on well with him.

To progress in the job, I had to take a promotion. They sent me north for a year to Butlin's holiday camp at Ayr, in Scotland, as the new bookings manager. In many ways it was like a sentence handed down by a magistrate. We had to rent out our lovely little house and spent a troublesome year in a dreary old place by the sea, called Girvan. I worked for the miserable and little Scottish general manager and his sour wife.

Our dumb dog Jason kept jumping over the wall and running off for the day. Jason's a soppy name for a dog and we really should have named him Randy. When we did get him back, he was knackered and so all he ever did was just sleep. Gail needed to do something other than look for the bloody dog. She answered a job advertisement and went to work in the Girvan Spa which disappointingly turned out to be a grocery shop.

Much of the time my job was taken up dealing with the complaints of Scottish working families, on holiday from nearby Glasgow. They were tough, no-nonsense people who all seemed to speak at once and in a strange tongue. The complaints were fairly consistent. Bed bugs, mould in the bathroom, condensation and just being cold. They would be quite angry, come in and start in on me straight away. They would say, "Hey, Jimmy, and then something, something, an dinny do. Do ya, ken?" Now if you don't understand this then, believe me neither did I.

I was now twenty-three and confident. It didn't help that Scottish people don't seem to like the English very much. We are constantly blamed for all their many problems. Dealing with angry people, being tall was a bit useful and I'm sure it helped me. I couldn't understand a word of what they were saying but learned to smile, be nice and listen carefully. Eventually, to make everyone feel more comfortable, I changed my name to Jimmy Robert Mardle and got the hang of the language. Surprisingly, I survived without injury. I certainly didn't want to upset these angry, down to earth, and very tough customers.

It wasn't all bad and the job wasn't so difficult and so I spent lots of my time organising coach trips for the staff to go to the Royal Edinburgh Military Tattoo and Loch Ness. Our parents came and went and so did Jason the dog. He went back with my mother and father who were far better suited to looking after him than we were.

It was when Gail's parents came to stay at the Turnberry hotel that I had my second go at horse riding and ice skating. I've always worked on the idea that if others can do it then it can't be so hard? We all went on a weekend trip to Aviemore. I don't properly remember how, but somehow Gail and I ended up going trekking on horseback. Gail, having been well brought up, had always ridden when she wasn't being a ballerina, so no problem for her. By this time, I was fluent in Scottish and thought, what can go wrong, I'll give it a go.

It's kind of funny but everything in Scotland is called 'The Highland' something or another. So, off we go and of course turned up at guess what? the 'Highland Stables'. The lady owner had a very posh voice, a very large bottom, and a set of sticky out teeth. She came out to greet us, eating a carrot, and with the oddest shaped legs I had ever seen. The tight trousers clung to her large bottom and her big thighs stuck out all sideways, in the shape of a half-moon. That of course made us giggle. She asked if I had ridden before and I of course replied, "Yes, sure, no problem." They took one look at me and because I was so tall, they decided Pansy, the sweet little horse chosen for me wasn't suitable. That I needed to ride a larger horse and so out came Hercules.

Gail's already mounted on a pretty little thing called Potty and without any fuss is ready to go. I'm now struggling to get my foot into the stirrup which is halfway up Hercules's ginormous middle. Once done, and with one foot in the cup, I'm now attached to the horse. He then starts wandering around leaving me to do a one-legged dance hopping all around the stable yard. It was one of those situations where you just don't have much of a choice other than to keep on going. The posh lady owner with the big bum, strange shaped legs and sticky out teeth was very nice and quickly stopped Hercules from having any more of his fun.

They then sent for some steps so I could get on. "OK," she says to me, "mount up." Easy-peasy, up onto the steps, foot in the stirrup, one bounce, and push. I went straight over the top and came down the other side which was funny but really not very cool! The carrot munching posh lady asked, "Are you sure you've done this before?"

Well off we go on this pony trekking malarky. I quickly worked out by watching everyone else, that when the horse goes down, *you* are supposed to go *up*. You then do the opposite. When the horse goes up, *you* then go *down*, all of this using just your knees.

Bloody hell, this wasn't easy. The soppy hat kept going over my eyes and Hercules wasn't doing anything I told him. I was being bounced and tossed around and thought that after this is all over, I would probably never be able to have any babies.

After an hour of this 'trekking' we were at last set to turn around and start making our way back the stables. This was the bit when I finally felt good. I pulled on the control strings and surprisingly Hercules turned around, looked up at me, smiled, farted and started heading back to home. The lady owner said to us in a posh horsey voice, "OK, we will now trot." Well, Hercules had clearly become bored and was fed up with messing me about. In reality he had just been waiting for this moment so he could get back to his bag of favourite munch, hanging on his peg back at the stables.

He reared up on his two back legs like he had seen Trigger do, when he was allowed to watch the *Lone Ranger* on the stable TV. He then took off at full speed. Everyone else but me seemed to be under control. At that moment, I was a bit like Roy Rogers' partner, Tonto, the Indian who had just lost control of the reins. I was flying along with the soppy hat over my eyes and with my arms just wrapped around this bloody horse's neck. Even as an un-accomplished jockey, I just knew we were in trouble and going for the stable short cut by jumping over the five-bar gate.

At the last minute, I was saved by the posh lady owner who with the legs like inflated air bags got safely between the gate and me. Using those air bags, she forced Hercules to turn away from the gate. After that, like a child, she took away the reins and wouldn't let me steer anymore. In disgrace, she led Hercules and me all the way back to the stable yard. She wasn't happy although I did explain that I had only ridden English horses before, and that this Scottish one was different!

After such a big adventure on day one, it was now day two and I went on to try my hand at ice skating. Now, as a kid I was seriously good on roller skates. At our block of flats at Priory Close, it was customary for the girls to stay home and learn to cook. Us boys on the other hand, were inventing new things like early days extreme sports. As well as extreme roller skating, a couple of things we came up with were stink bomb making and DIY building your own explosives. To participate in these extreme sports, you had to be able to run fast, especially in the case of the explosives, so it was all really quite healthy.

In chemistry classes they taught us at school how to blow glass using a Bunsen burner. You melted the end of the glass tube and blew down the cold end to make a glass bubble. When it cooled you could fill it with a concoction of acid and certain zinc type metal fillings. It really stunk, like the smell of really bad eggs. No one said you couldn't do this at home and so we did. Having learned the basics at school we did our own homework. Using the gas pipe that came out of the wall to melt and seal the end of the glass bubbles, we made our own very useful stink bombs. They were very good, and we could drop them in the newly invented shops called supermarkets or just down the stairwells in the middle of the next block of flats.

The other bit of useful ordinance was to take an old aluminium cigar tube and fill it up with weed killer and fertiliser that you could get from the hardware shop around the corner. You had to mix it very carefully on the floor, so it didn't self-ignite. Then squash it very gently into the tube and use the fuse from a firework banger through a hole in the top. This was all led by Bertie Preston, the neighbourhood tough guy, who lived at number forty-six. Once it was dark, he would take these loaded cigar tins down the back of the flats and blow up pretty much anything that the Germans had missed, wooden tree stumps and the laundry lines. Now, being older and a lot wiser, I realise how terribly dangerous this really all was. Bertie of course went on to join the SAS.

Back to roller skating, which started by our learning to

stand up on skates, in the hallway on the ground floor, without falling over. The hallways were smooth polished concrete and so were the best place to start. To begin with it was very funny as you looked like you were tap dancing and unable to stop. Once you had cracked that, it was off outside to the nearest hill. The skates were held on with shoelaces that went halfway up your legs which at that age wasn't very far. You soon learned to do them up tight so that nothing wobbled around. The trouble with that was your feet went numb and you lost all feeling in your legs. It sort of didn't matter as gravity just took over. The faster you went the easier it became to control the skates going down hills.

Once we had mastered the stopping bit, which usually meant chucking yourself into a bush, we moved onto bigger things. To start with this meant hanging onto the milk float as it went along. Trouble with that was Ernie used to get the hump quite quickly. You had to let go or he would start throwing out-of-date yoghurts at you.

Roller Skate Graduation and Hall of Fame recognition was achieved by hanging onto the pole, on the open platform, at the back of the number twelve double-decker school bus. The conductor was usually busy selling tickets and packets of five Woodbine cigarettes to all us school kids. It always took a while before he saw you and came looking for your ticket. Success was measured by how many stops you made before getting busted.

The startup technique for ice skating was the same as roller skating. It was only when you put the skates with blades on for the first time you realised the difference. I was always trying to impress Gail and her mother. So once kitted up I was off. I clung onto everything and anyone as I got onto the ice. I soon came to realise that like roller skating, the faster you went the more you seemed to be under control. Once again, my newly acquired and useful Scots language skills came into play as I shouted out,

"Hey, Jimmy, di ye no ken me," before knocking over lots of very angry 'Highland' Scots people with painted blue faces. It was very similar to ten pin bowling only on this occasion, I was the ball!

Falling over on the ice is bad enough if you're wearing jeans. These Scots numpties ended up sliding along, on the freezing cold ice, sitting on their squashed testicles and big hairy bums. No wonder they were happy to see us go. The in-laws were seeing a whole new side of me and once again.

I don't think Gail, or her mother were very impressed.

Being in the world of Rivett was good. Richard, Gail's brother, was now the MD running his father's business with Jim taking a back seat as chairman. All very correct and formal. Richard did all the work and Jim would sit in his top floor office behind his big green leather desk. To enter the chairman's office, you had to press a button. On the wall was a traffic light system of red, amber, and green. Once you got the green light in you went and Jim, all serious and businesslike, would be sitting there in his suit, covered in cigarette ash.

Rivett's never worked for other people. They went to boarding schools, played rugby, and ran their own companies. I will always be grateful as they treated me as an equal and always made me feel like I should be like them. Richard convinced me that at my age, I should have a plan. At that point in my life, I of course didn't know I had to have one. Working for yourself sounded like a good idea and since so many other people did it, I decided to give it a try and to run my own game.

With no GCSEs and only a Boy Scouts badge for sewing, and a cycling proficiency badge, I was struggling to come up with an obvious route to success. When the catering college wrote to tell me not to come back, they kindly sent me a City and Guilds cooking certificate, which of course was very helpful. So very slowly a plan started to take shape. Learn how it all works, get a restaurant and easy, Bob's your uncle and off you go. I blame Richard for this flawed line of thinking.

With commitment and determination, we once again, launched ourselves in this new direction. We quit our safe Scottish jobs and were repatriated back to England. The only difference being that this time, I didn't have to give up my passport. To learn the trade and obtain the required knowledge, I applied for a job abroad, well I thought Guernsey was abroad. In 1974, I became the second chef at the very French sounding Moulin Huet Hotel in Guernsey. It all sounded very chic, and I assumed very continental. This was going to help my career, build my CV and inspire me. I soon found out that shepherd's pie was very popular along with roast lamb, ice cream and apple crumbles. So much for French Cuisine.

With little else to do, poor Gail who had by now been married to me for three years, was to become a chambermaid which wasn't ideal. The funny thing I recall is that most of time she was really quite happy. She hated the job, which was never in her wildest dreams on her list of things to do or become. It meant to her horror she was too close to the other girls. They smoked roll ups, slurped their cups of tea and worst of all, at the morning break, didn't cut their toast in half. She did however like lying out in the sun, every afternoon, in our private little garden house. Without knowing it, this had to be a taste of the future although we didn't get too carried away. It was a small room, with a wash basin tucked away in the corner, located somewhere quietly at the back of the private garden.

The Channel Islands are amazing and the weather in 1974 was so good. I worked breakfast, lunch, and dinner. I also worked in the bar during the evenings for extra cash. Funnily enough this suited Gail as well. It would all be over by 10pm and the residents, full of Kate and Sidney pie, were all done in. She would happily join in, keeping me company sipping free Babychams all night long. It all kind of worked out as things so often do. Before you knew it, Gail had the perfect suntan and we had amazingly made a baby Ben. With that great news, it was July and time to go back home to Aldbury.

A Life in the Toilets

We had not long returned home from working in Guernsey for the summer. Once we were back in England, with a bun in the oven, I needed to get a job quickly. Having just left one hotel kitchen I felt very well qualified to apply for a labourer's job, building a New hotel kitchen at Hemel Hempstead. The site manager, Harry, thought this was funny and so gave me the start.

The job involved carrying bricks up ladders and running wheelbarrow loads of concrete around, which if you've never tried it, is really hard work. So, after a while and with my unusual cooking skills, a boy scouts cooking badge and a city and guilds cooking certificate, I applied and ended up working in the hotel kitchen, as the sous chef, making sauces and soups every day.

It was time to take stock of things. It's 1974 and the swinging sixties were over. So, there we were, married with a baby Ben in production. We have a mortgage and a lovely little house, in a gorgeous country village. I'm a Morris dancer, and not many people can say that. We have a Mini Countryman car and a motorbike. We have a good social life, a few nice new friends, and a tiny black and white TV with a high-tech coat hanger shoved up its bottom. We lived a few doors down from a village pub, and we were happy, sorted, and ready to take on the next of life's challenges.

I think this was the time that everything changed for us. The lovely little house was not big enough and it was time to move on to a £14,000 three-bedroomed house that had a fridge freezer, in High Wycombe. We had our own back garden beach with a pond, a sandpit, and a real time Desmond the duck. Gail had another one in the oven (Claire) and was already being a super mum, sunbathing in the hottest summer on record and not going back to work any time soon.

I was still working as a chef because someone had told me that, to open a restaurant, this is what I had to do. It was while mending, in the months after the 'bike crash of 1975' that the bleedin'

obvious kicked in. Only posh boys, from posh schools and posh families, can even think they have a chance at starting their own businesses. People like me just have to get on with a 'proper job' and serve the posh peoples. I was told to focus on what we were good at and so we had made Claire.

The insurance company had compensated me for the campervan driver, who had tried to kill me. While mending, following the accident, looking out of the window my neighbour, and now lifelong friend Rob Cavell, used to come and go to work each day dressed as Robby the Rep. He wore a suit, shirt, and tie, which I didn't even own. He drove a nice, big, yellow company car with a 'sunroof'. He left home after breakfast and came home every day at teatime, closing the 'sunroof' before getting out of his Ford Capri. What a difference my life was. Split shifts, getting home at midnight, working weddings for overtime and a car without a sunroof. It was time for a career change.

I was just as good as he was and if he could do this then so could I. So, as Robby the Rep 2, I read the Situations Vacant ads in the newspapers, and went after as many as fifty sales representative jobs. I learned quickly, getting the hang of job interviews. It was in 1975 that Odex, a cleaning chemicals manufacturer, recognised me as being a star in the making. They told me I wouldn't need luncheon vouchers as "we don't stop for lunch." They did pay a basic wage but really you had to hit the targets and then you got the all-important bonus. Once we all agreed, they sent me to pick up the company car (didn't have a sunroof!) and for two weeks' sales training in Cheshire with a super bloke called Frank Moss. Now, how brave were they.

I loved it. Frank was a great trainer, and I took to it like Desmond did to our garden pond. I was trained in how to do the job, given a huge suitcase full of samples and eight hundred customers to look after in and around Oxfordshire. We were expected to make twenty face-to-face customer calls a day. We were targeted to make eight orders a day and the company manufactured the products as well as delivered the orders. My sales manager, Bob Glennie, was a great motivator and an inspirational manger. In the whole company there were eighty sales reps just like me.

Maybe the difference was I was younger, happy, drove the car faster and needed the bonuses more. I learned to push and go that little bit further. I made twenty-one calls and ten orders

a day. I remember how often, on the way home, stopping to make just one more call. The end result was bigger bonuses and becoming the salesman of the year. I proudly won a great big trophy presented at the annual sales conference in front of the whole company. Since I was costing them so much money in bonuses, was such a cocky sod, and could read and write I was promoted to an being an area manager. I was now working an area from Norfolk across to Bristol, being responsible for myself and a team of eight sales reps. Thank god for the Pee and Tea, AA road book.

It went well and it was a big part in how we came to be running our own show. Big companies couldn't continue to run large sales teams or to deliver £50-£100 orders direct to the people who used the products. So, on behalf of the company, I became part of setting up a network of distributors. Small local companies who would cost effectively process and deliver the company's orders.

One day in 1978, working with Bennie the rep in Reading, I had seen an estate agents shop window selling new houses in nearby Binfield. They had four bedrooms and *two* bathrooms, one being *en-suite*. Wow, now I had forgotten about car sunroofs,

this was the mutt's nuts and a bargain at only £22,000. No question it was a must-do thing. We went along to have a look taking Claire, our number two Mini Monster with us. It wasn't her fault, but we weren't paying attention and somehow Claire destroyed the show house by knocking down all their soppy signs. The agent and Claire were both upset and started crying. The sales lady had probably been to the same Frank Moss school of selling, as me. She quickly recovered, stuck her false eyelashes back on, and told us we had broken everything and that we now had to buy the house. So, we did, and got out quick.

Binfield, 1977 was our first new home and, along with every move in our young lives, we had unconsciously raised our game. We were among PLUs (people like us); hardworking, aspiring middle class young parents. As we come and go through life, we are always meeting new people. Some leave a big and lasting impression. It was during this time that we met Patsie and Otto who, along with Mike and Marilyn, became lifetime friends as well as godparents to our children.

With them, as well as playing space invaders down at the pub, we put on Christmas parties in the village hall and held street parties. We had house parties, dinners, went to theatres, concerts, and balls. We met many of their friends, some we still keep in touch with forty-five years on.

On the way home from work each day I would stop and read the paper in the local pub, the Victoria Arms. The landlord, Mick, was an all right young man, the beer was good, and I fell

in with all the wrong people. I become very good friends with Eddie the loud, extrovert roof tiler and his crew. Before long I ended up playing five-a-side football and staying up all night in the pub doing lockdowns. A lockdown was when the pub locked the doors and you settled down with the landlord just hanging out, laughing, and drinking until the brewery lorry turned up at 6.30am. You couldn't help but like Eddie and his mates and he liked us. (He still owes me £350 for bailing him out of Reading jail after he was arrested for some punch up or another.)

We were just into our thirties when we had a go at some serious bike riding. You never had to ask Eddie twice, he was always up for anything. We both talked Gail into joining in with the 65,000 other contestants on the 1980 London to Brighton bike ride.

We were doing this marathon ride with Eddie and Jo, his squeeze. One of the first mistakes we made was choosing to do the event on a tandem. They were just so heavy. People think two people on one bike means half the work. In hiring tandems, we discovered two hours after setting off, that this wasn't true. One person is always doing the peddling while the other one is out of sync or just taking a nap. The second mistake was finding just outside London, a Fuller's pub selling our favourite beer. Stopping for a couple of beers turned out to be a bad idea. It was so hot and as the miles went on, we struggled more and more. We were knackered.

Sixty-five thousand participants were a big deal. The crowds, lining the seventy-mile route, were shouting us on, throwing flowers and spraying champagne as we rode past. That was until we got to this bloody great hill at Ditchling in the middle of Sussex. It was all well and good that the ducks and geese just flew over the top of this mountain. We couldn't fly and with ten miles still to go we couldn't walk let alone ride. Somehow with true grit and a chocolate Marathon bar, we manged to walk up to the top. From there we could see, in the distance, the sun reflecting off the orchestra at the finish line in Brighton. It was all downhill from that point on.

I find it ironic that the whole event was put on and run by the British Heart Foundation. I guess back in 1980 they were just short of customers and trying to make a point: exercise kills.

I don't think we were the last but having come somewhere

near the end, we collected our medals and rode into the Ship hotel's underground garage. We couldn't walk, our thighs were rubbing together, and our bums were very sore. From there we had to crawl up two flights of very steep stairs and to the amusement of everyone in reception crawl across the carpet to the check in desk. They were very good and instantly seeing the problem, allocated us two disabled persons' rooms.

Now we knew what it was all about, Eddie and I did the event again the following year. We rented two very nice lightweight bikes and stayed away from the Fuller's drinks stop. Like a pair of maniacs, we did the race in two and a half hours and then we had a few beers. For a while we really got into peddling around. As well as another London to Brighton we rode off to Cambridge and the legendary three counties.

Bankrupted Mini Monsters

Our own mini monsters, Ben and Claire, were consuming more and more food as well as looking very trendy in Mothercare's co-ordinating clothes. In the fast-changing times, I was twenty-eight and getting job offers to come and work with the new distributors we had set up. It was a difficult choice, but we had little to lose, and there was a lot more money to be earned if we changed jobs.

I became self-employed, bought myself a car and went to work as an agent for a local company called Adams of Camberley. It was a simple arrangement where I didn't get paid a basic wage, but I was paid a high commission for whatever I sold on my area, which was central London.

I answered to the sales manager who was very out of date as well as being a bit of a boozer. He had a big red pockmarked nose and trousers that wouldn't do up. What a surprise, I didn't like being told what to do and he didn't like me. We quickly fell out and he fired me. I was quite used to being fired before I was married but this time, with a wife and two children, it was different, and I really needed the job.

I worked out that being a distributor was quite simple. You bought stock from a supplier, shoved it into a warehouse and then sold it to a customer. You then made sure you recorded the sale in the good book and made sure you got paid the money. How hard can that be? and I thought, I could do this. So, in a bit of a rush, I did. I already had the customers all around the West End of London. All I needed was some money, a warehouse, some stock, a phone number, and a van.

Once again, the patron saint of cleaners, Saint Mopalot, came to my rescue. A beam of light shone down from the sky onto Amen Corner close to where we lived in Binfield. This then, in the mud, amongst all the wrecked cars and vans, was where, for me, it all started. A big old wooden shed which I quickly fitted out using a big hammer, lots of nails and plenty of old wood which was lying around. I used one of the big, nearby, national suppliers for stock and their drivers were helpful. They were also very good at getting stuck in the mud on a regular basis. We somehow got by and made it all work.

My father-in-law Jim had helped by selling me a good but old Murray's van. Working and setting up distributors for Odex had taught me what customers wanted, where and what to buy. We muddled along and every day during the week I would get out there, all around central London, and generate the orders. We bought four-part invoices from WH Smith's and Gail typed them up and wrote up the good books.

On Saturdays, little Ben and I loaded up the wagon, and we went about doing all the deliveries from the week's work. Ben, aged four, used to help lugging and shoving the boxes in the door. He used to get given tips which went towards his first taste of a McDonalds. This was 1978 and McD's had only just been invented. We were already living the dream, and this was Ben's idea of how it was meant to be. Once the work was done, on the way home, he would sit on a box of toilet rolls in the back of the van. Using another box as a table for his milk shake, burger and chips he would make out as a perfectly happy chappie.

The accountant showed me how to keep basic books. We

needed a trading name, and my mum suggested our name backwards. That worked, and so in 1978 we came to be Seldram Supplies, and so it was. I was young and strong, and we both worked very hard. Gail looked after the little monsters, and I took care of earning the money. The business grew quickly, and so did our family. We never looked back.

As well as being a muddy bog, Amen Corner quickly became too small for what we were selling. Seldram Supplies had to move to a bigger unused chicken shed on a nearby local pig farm. George, the owner, and our new landlord was a bit of a terrifying drunk and so were his pigs. As is the way with travellers, he and his family had graduated from being caravan owners to another of life's contradictions, a mobile home.

Let's be honest here, they weren't mobile. They were propped up on a pile of bricks and like every other homeowner, connected to all the services. The problem was whose services were they connected to. You could often follow the electric powerline back to a nearby lamp post! They were a big family, very well known locally and a bit frightening. I was always straight with them and paid the rent in £5 drinking vouchers, which always made George very happy. On a good day he was very helpful and was OK with me.

The worst part of all this was when you came into the warehouse at the start of the day. You never knew what you were going find. Sometimes George would still be very drunk and slumped in a corner somewhere. There would be glass and wreckage everywhere. The TV and the kitchen fridge would be in the garden and the windows in the 'mobile home' would need replacing again. His car would be stuck, somewhere in the field, with the engine still running, and the pigs and chickens would be running around everywhere.

It was the snorting, biting pigs that we were most afraid of. They got into the shed and chased after us when we were trying to get going and to load the van. The pooping machines that were the chickens, weren't such a problem. It was Don the driver's idea that we hang a bunch of cooking apples on the front door to frighten away the pigs. For the chickens, we found that by waving packets of Paxo stuffing at them it would get them all out of the warehouse before we had to leave every day. We decided that with many more people becoming vegetarians, there were just more and more chickens and pigs to have to deal with.

To our great surprise Rebecca had popped out into our world. This meant Gail was even more busy than before. It became clear that I was now number four in the food chain and that the children were far more important than me. That was OK as I think we both had our hands full, only in different ways. The business was booming, neither of us had ever heard of Thomas, and we were quite fond of falling asleep on the sofa.

By this time, we were becoming a proper business. I took a lease on a shop on the very busy Vauxhall Bridge Road, just down from Central London's Victoria railway station. My friend Rob Cavell and I fitted it out using a big hammer, lots of bits of wood and some more nails. I think they were all leftovers

from the first attempt at the warehouse at Amen Corner. The business had already grown, and the phone had started to ring. I needed to employ some help to answer the phone, take the orders and start keeping the books. I bought our first computer, learned to use it and so it became our first proper office and a trade counter selling ten rolled up black bags for a pound to anyone who wanted to buy.

I got lucky in those booming years. 1978 to 1987 things were changing fast helped along by hyper-inflation. It was like a new generation of post-war baby boomers had popped out of the ground and come alive. Things were happening very quickly, and everything looked different. That same generation of people had now become producers as well as the consumers. We were greedy, in a hurry and impatient. If we wanted something and it didn't exist, then someone would invent it, make it, or come up with it. There was a bloke called Freddy Laker who invented airplane travel so cheap that you contemplated flying to work every day instead of taking the train. Another geezer, called Alan Sugar, who invented a way of sending toilet paper to each other through a telephone machine. For me it was a case of being in the right place at the right time, working hard and having the balls to go in through the back door. That way you got to speak with the people that mattered and not necessarily the self importants upstairs. The business grew quickly and successfully, and it was a good time to be around.

I had moved the warehouse from the out-of-London pig farm, which by now was surrounded by animal activists, to railway arches at the top of the Vauxhall Bridge Road. We became like Hobbits living in 8,000sq feet of storage under the main line running into Waterloo railway station. We opened a new company, the London Numatic Sales Service and Parts centre on the Albert Embankment. It looked amazing and was a great advertisement for our growing business. Steve Tibbles (named after our cat) ran that side of our company selling and

repairing Henry hoovers and cleaning machines from our first showroom.

After a few years I went back and bought the Adams of Camberley business from where all this started. This then became Seldram Supplies (Aldershot). It was with real pleasure that on day one, I fired the large and alcoholic sales manager with the red nose. With this addition we acquired some really good people. This enabled us to move into a decent warehouse in Farnborough and open our second trade counter.

After my first tour in 1976 as "Robby the Rep 2", I always felt good about Oxfordshire. It's a lovely county of rolling hills and chalk downs. It's classic England with its stone-built villages. The people of Oxfordshire were clearly ready for two- and three-ply soft toilet rolls. So, in 1986 I went back to my old territory, and started a new operation right in the centre of the city, Seldram Supplies (Oxford). As a start-up, it was down to me to put it all together and to make it happen.

I rented a warehouse and once again got out the hammer and nails to make a trade counter. I bought an enormous, ex-building site, porta-cabin for an office. This turned up complete with 3 builders inside still having a nap after their tea break. This was the warehouse that one weekend, Rebecca, aged ten, and I completely fitted out with racking. We behaved like a right pair of monkeys swinging from the top of the uprights, sliding down to the bottom, climbing up the ladders and balancing on the beams. I would haul them up and hold them and she would bash 'em in with the company hammer. Great job 'Magic Magoo'.

I must have been doing something right since by 1986, I started getting other companies come along wanting to buy us. The money in those days was crazy and the offers just kept piling up until eventually, aged thirty-six, I just couldn't say no.

The sale of all the companies was managed by Mr Andrews, our then tubby little Welsh accountant, who was better at stuffing his face than selling a company. This was when the bubble popped! What did I know about selling a company. I sold toilet rolls and depended on him. He was completely out of his depth, and he turned out to be all size and no substance. Unbeknown at the time, our gambling gay, alcoholic, admin manager was stealing money from us in a very clever way. Our tubby accountant should have verified the debtors, confirming who owed us money and that the books balanced. He never did. Things weren't adding up and he just wasn't smart enough to see it. It wasn't until the sale of the company had completed that the buyer's accountants found it out and stuck me with the problem.

The companies' value had been overstated and resulted in my breaching the contract and losing the final six figure payment of the purchase contract. The sale itself was simple but all wrongly set up. I knew nothing of these things and had to rely on our useless Welsh accountant. From the start, the sale was structured wrongly which resulted in my eventually paying a quarter million pounds in capital gains tax – OUCH! I often wonder why then, after a year of Highland hospitality. Having the government threatening to send my family and I to Australia for non-payment of taxes, I've still got a bag on with both the Welsh and The Scots.

The case was clear, so taking advice I sued the doughnut look-alike, Mr Yaky-Dah bloody Andrews, who was of course insured for this sort of thing. It was a pretty clear case. As is the way between the solicitors, barristers, and accountants it all fell apart on the steps of the courthouse. They got paid and I didn't.

The tax bill from the Inland Revenue was now a big and an unexpected problem. Following the sale, I had become involved in some dodgy property developments. People you meet just love to tell you how they had bought property. Done it all up and sold it on for a huge profit during what was then a booming property market. Once again, I thought, well if they can do it, so can I. This then was another of life's hard learned lessons when along came what they called Black Friday, when everything went tits up.

As well as big financial crash, along came the Inland Revenue wanting their money. I tried paying them off, every year, over a couple of years. What they didn't care about was we also had to pay the school fees, which, at the time trumped the IRS. We had invested in some properties and had always bought and sold our houses wisely. This then meant there was equity in what we had. They had no patience and were behaving like a bunch of Raptors from Jurassic park. That meant a day trip to the seaside enforcement office at Worthing where they happily smiled and told me they had decided I should pay the whole amount, NOW. Once they stopped smiling, they turned out to be not very nice and said, "Pay up or we will bankrupt you." We didn't hang around for fish and chips that day!

We had to sell the house with the swimming pool and to take a time out, living at a new house around the corner at the Pavilions End. We weren't cricket fans and the house had next-door neighbours, no fortress wall, or big gates. They called it 'open plan' and there was no garden that you could do anything with, and you parked on the drive, in front of the garage.

The bank wasn't happy and nor was Her Majesty's Inland Revenue. The property values had all dropped, borrowing cost more and, for the time being, the boom was over. For a while we had a mad scramble around to find enough cash needed to pay off the government. It was either that or take a one-way holiday to the end of the world. I got a bit lucky and ended up doing some sort of dodgy deal at Lloyds bank's regional office. It was a bit like playing Monopoly with the kids. They repossessed the Wellingtonia Vintners shop I had bought in exchange for the debt. The investment house in Park Road got finished and sold. Because of the property crash it didn't deliver and to cap it all, we lost money on that as well. Those people we had met, who are so quick to tell you how much they made, and never tell you about those deals that didn't! Another life lesson, stick to what you know.

So, it was only for a short while until we sorted things out and recovered. The six of us were happy, life was still hard work but still good. We made a few bob by selling the cricketers house and quickly moved on.

Needless to say, sucking up the lessons learned, I changed accountants going to a bigger local practice where they had experts in the various elements. After some ten years they got me into a situation where they repeatedly failed to answer routine requests from HMRC. These were simple enquiries into aspects of my business, tax returns and incomes. Eventually HMRC decided that they had had enough of being ignored and used their muscle to get what they wanted.

Believe me if you've never been there. This is scary stuff. These guys are the ultimate bean counters, and they really love nothing more than your telephone bill or your year-on-year petrol expenses. This resulted in a full-blown investigation into all and every aspect of our tax affairs over seven years. They say, if you leave the door open… That cost me a lot of money since I hadn't ever heard of 'pecuniary interest' and probably nor had the accountants who I had once again trusted.

I always get a bit put out when people tell me I can't afford something that I want. In 1998 we found and bought the best house on a private estate in Tekels Park, Camberley. It overlooked a fifty-acre meadow which was surrounded by woodland. This fabulous looking house was our seventh mortgage in 27 years. I had by now learned that you can work the numbers to get a mortgage but not to pay your capital gains tax bill. I remember out walking with my mum and dad through the meadow one afternoon. From a distance asking them if they liked it and then proudly telling them we had bought the house they were looking at.

We were back in the game.

To Ski or Not to Ski

Loads of people we knew would go skiing each year. My sleeping partner had of course been skiing since she was four. No worries, I signed up for ski lessons on the world-famous dry ski slope at Bracknell. Let's face it, I thought, it can't be that hard, loads of people do it. Admittedly we were only a few days away from going on my first winter adventure with our friends Mike, Marilyn, and some of their older children. We went to a place called Obergurgl in Austria.

The flight into and out of Salzburg is super crazy. You flew on a small four engine passenger jet converted from an ex-military plane. The pilot clearly believes in life after death. It dives into the valleys between the mountains. To help keep you calm, the cabin staff ran around giving you extra shots of Appel Schnapps as the engines roared like an Apollo space rocket. The flight swerves around the peaks before diving back into the valleys. If you had a window seat you could see the wings flapping and the flames coming out of the engines on full afterburners. It was worth the trip just for the flight.

After a few more years of head planting and generally crashing out, I thought I had the hang of this skiing caper. In fact, I was so confident that every year, we took and taught our children who can now all ski really well. Each year, around Gail's birthday, we would also all go in one big group of friends to France in a catered chalet in the Three Valleys. There are just so many funny stories that come from our time skiing. You should have been there!

The after dinner indoor fireworks on the dining room table. David lighting such a big fire in the chalet Grand Tetras that the chimney cracked. In the fire shack of a restaurant dancing on the table, in the middle of dinner, with big Ray. Fancy dress murder mysteries where everyone dressed up big time. Skiing home from the Rond Point après ski parties in the dark. Christmas Eve 1997 after dinner, up on the mountain, with all my family tobogganing back down the mountain on an upside-down table. At mid-night, in a Tignes French ski apartment, when Bobbie jumped up onto the top bunk to get into bed. The whole thing, including Bobbie, collapsed down on top of me trying to get to sleep in the bottom bunk.

In all those years of skiing, one particular day stands out more than the rest. It was one morning in Courchevel, and we were a group of four skiers: Gail, me and two teenagers. We were finding our own way around the mountain when we came to a great big, giant mogul field leading down the piste.

Mogul fields are sort of created from lots of good off-piste snow, not touched, or prepared by the piste-bashing machines. It's really mountain moles that do all the hard work. They push up from below to create a carpet of giant snowy bubbles. You're supposed to ski around all the bumps, turning, bending zee knees, turning, and turning again as you go down the hill. It's all a bit tricky but we were generally OK with this.

We all hesitated at the top, which you really shouldn't do. Big and brave, I go first crossing form left to right and back again. A little rhythm is very important here. I don't properly remember what happened but somehow, someone else not in our group, crossed in front of me and I stopped on the top of a bump. Next thing I knew was that I went backwards, slipped, and fell. That was it, game over, and I was on my way. Over the bumps, around the bumps, rolling and tumbling down the mountain.

I knew it was important and managed to get rid of one ski, but the other just wouldn't release. Everything seemed to slow down and even my thoughts were running in slow motion through my head. Even though it was like being beaten up, at the time you only feel the physical impacts and not the pain. I understood that whatever happens, to prevent injury, you must try and stay calm, relaxed and not to tense up. That you must get rid of the other ski, or it will break your leg. I passed under the busy ski lift, which at that moment was more like a grandstand, with all the people watching. I rolled, bumped, and bounced all the way down to the road. I clearly remember thinking this is good and it will now stop. It didn't and I went straight across the road and carried on down the other side.

After a total of 300 metres, I eventually stopped and just lay there for a long while. Gradually, I discovered that I hadn't broken anything although I felt bashed and bruised all over. It hadn't looked promising from the top and the others who then gradually came down to help. I think we were all in shock. However, the show must go on and I just needed to be left alone for an hour to recover. Gail and the boys were very shaken up by the whole experience.

A man came up to me at lunchtime and said he had watched it all from the chair lift. How unbelievable it was to walk away from that accident. That I was clearly a very lucky man and should go buy a lottery ticket as soon as possible. A lot of alcohol was drunk at lunch that day.

Unbelievably, the day wasn't over. We're still on the mountain and, as the saying goes. "When you fall off the horse, you're best to get straight back on." I suppose that this applies to skiing as well. I was bumped, bashed, and bruised but other than that, OK. After a few sherbets and now feeling very refreshed! Gail and I gently set off, on our own, to get back down to the chalet. We hadn't gone far when, one after the other, we jumped over a small little jump. Gail crashed out which is something she never does. Giggle giggle, ha ha seniors, but… she couldn't stand up. Her knee had parted company with the top of her leg and there started the afternoon's performance.

It was obvious that we needed the St John's ambulance and that we didn't have their number. Gail was kind of OK, already anaesthetised, not in a lot of pain, but not able to use her left leg in any way. The best way to get off the mountain in cases like this is on the blood wagon. This means zooming down the slopes with two very fit geezers, no poles, and an all-weather arctic sledge. The ever-helpful Gail refused and insisted *we* climb back up the slope to the ski lift and then get help.

It was the '*we*' bit that was now my problem. It hadn't been my best day after having already completed three rounds fighting with the Gypsy King. I know had to carry Gail *up* a mountain in ski boots and in knee deep soft snow. It took a very long time, but in the end I did it. Leaving her propped up on a seat I then had to go all the way back down the bloody slope and fetch back two sets of skis, poles, gloves and of course don't forget the lip balm.

Four hours after lunch we get to the doctors and an X-Ray which then led to a trip, with credit card in hand, to the hospital at Moutier. They were very good and put me in one bed and Gail in the other. I was all in and so was Gail.

We both spent the next week with me going backwards and forwards to and from the hospital with takeaway meals and essential stuff. After the operation the insurers flew Gail home. She had some new bits in her knee, a pair of crutches and the highway code for wheelchair users. I had the car and had to go home alone. Somewhere near Agincourt where, after Crecy, the Brits gave the French another good bashing, the bleedin' French police did an exclusive, motorway time over distance thing on the British drivers. They waited as you came through the autoroute exit booth. Having paid your money, they were looking for a British number plate and then they pounced. They were so not very helpful especially after I mentioned the local history, the battlefield and asked did they ever take up archery? I only just had enough cash to pay the bill. They just couldn't care less. Without the cash, they would have impounded the car and made me walk.

There's always an up and a downside to things. The upside was that for six months, with Gail in a wheelchair, we got to go straight to the front of any queues. The downside was that for six months I got to do all the shopping and the cooking.

My skiing history goes much the same way. At my last attempt at snow skiing, we were somewhere up a mountain in Swiss Flims. We're hanging out with some of the members of the legendary Cirque du Berlinger, William, Elliot, and Oscar. Both Gail and I, of course, have our own ski equipment which we bought in 1996. The boots no longer fitted properly, and the skis are made from recycled bits of the Concorde. I wasn't feeling comfortable right from the start. At 2,500 metres we got off the chair lift. It takes a while 'to find your ski legs' which of course were still firmly attached to my bottom.

I don't know why but I was really struggling to remain in control of my skis. It was probably due to my age, weight, and the lack of oxygen. Instead of leading the pack I now found myself following all the little nippers as they blasted down the mountain, jumping, going backwards, zigzagging, and generally showing off. The thing is when you lose your bottle skiing down a piste, you know you're in trouble. I'm managing to get down to 2,000 metres when gravity takes over and things start to speed up. The trail we were on starts narrowing and there are more and more skiers getting in everyone's way.

Now, I've skied for thirty years or so and I reckon I was pretty good at it. On this particular day I was lucky if I could even stand up without just falling over for more than five minutes. There is always soft snow and fewer people out at the edges of a run. You could say that I was skilfully traversing the piste, going from one side to the other. Although on that day this wasn't true. My boots had finally given up. I still couldn't find my ski legs and the uncontrollable skis just kept wobbling around all over the place. At the bottom of this run there were a series of bends. There's a slatted wooden fence down one side. The larger gaps between

had all the red criss-cross tape to stop you taking the fast route to the bottom of the mountain. Your brain quickly processes all this information and then tells you, you're in trouble.

I ended up being upside down with one leg and one ski sticking out of the fence, and the rest of me wrapped up in all the red tape. I didn't, but Oscar and the boys thought it was all very funny as they tried to find my other ski and pull me and my ski poles out of the wreckage. I left my skis at the bottom of the mountain and my boots in the hotel locker. It was fun while it lasted.

Gail wasn't impressed.

All For One

Gail's and my time together and what we have achieved has been amazing and rightly, something we can be very proud of. Our four children and the way we brought them up. The love and the bond that still exists between them, as well as us parents, is something very special.

It's not like cake making from a recipe book. With parenting you're getting into something that you seriously have no idea about. You have no training, no experience, and to be fair, you have no idea of what's about to hit you. The best you can do is to cling onto Fanny Haddocks or Gina Ford's handbook on how to raise a baby and hope for the best.

To pay the bills I had to go to work and was very busy grafting for long hours building a new business. Gail was the perfect 'Mummy'. She was kind, patient and loved her children and just seemed to take it all in her stride. It was like she had found *her* place in the great scheme of things. She just proudly took to being a mummy, like it was always meant to be.

I think we both found ourselves doing what we were really good at, and it became the making of both of us. As the family grew so did we, simply accepting and reacting to the changes as we needed. Ben first and then, when Claire came along, a bigger house. We moved house three times in seven years ending up in a five-bedroomed farmhouse with some acres, stables, and just what we needed, an all-weather dressage arena!

We were lucky in that the work was going well and we were in a good place to make one of the best decisions we ever made. Right from the start we chose to give the children the best education we could afford.

Ben being oldest was always the guinea pig and the first to make the step up to big school. The longer hours at a private school made for a long day and so aged thirteen, he asked to become a boarder at Bearwood College. The girls were already at a really good day school, the Marist Convent at Ascot. On Mondays to Fridays, they caught the 8am coach and returned around 5pm every day to do their homework while sat in front of the TV watching *Home and Away* and *Neighbours*.

All this in turn meant that little Thomas, aged eight, always seemed to get the short straw. His day was 08am to 6pm Monday to Friday and Saturday until midday. His school was a lovely, very informal day/boarding school. Run by a Mr and Mrs Paterson. It was a feeder school for Wellington College named after the Duke of Wellington who was of course the inventor of Wellington Boots. It catered for away-from-home army types who were posted abroad and wanted a stable family environment for young aspiring boarders wanting to get into Wellingtons.

The girls were growing up and the amount of homework they had to do meant they were kept pretty well occupied. Eventually we made the decision to make Thomas into a weekly boarder. For him, time at home was a bit lonely, short, and not really much fun. By becoming a weekly boarder, he got the most out of all the school activities as well as being surrounded by his friends. He was then free to come home every Saturday lunchtime and all-day Sunday, joining in with us and the two girls.

At sixteen, Rebecca had her own plans. Wellington College would take her, but it had some issues. Because she lived nearby and couldn't play rugby, they would only take her as a day pupil. She wanted to become a boarder which, in her case, we thought to be a good idea. Rebecca, otherwise known as Magic Magoo, was always a good girl, helping out wherever she could. By being smart and getting a two-year scholarship to Bradfield College, which was somewhere out in Hampshire, this helped me enormously. That meant they paid half the fees and me and the Inland Revenue paid the rest. Paying four lots of school fees was always very exciting. You knew they were coming at the start of each term. What I never knew was where the money was coming from. There were a few times when I had to ring up and explain that the wheels on the bus had actually come off and we were still waiting for the garage to come and fix them.

What wasn't very nice was when the Inland Revenue were threatening to bankrupt me. The bloke, who was very busy turning me over, took great pride in explaining what 'pecuniary interest' was. When you write a company cheque to the school to pay the school fees, you are creating a personal loan to the director. So that, for him, was a 'Gotcha moment'. One nil to the IRS who now wanted me to pay interest on all the school fees the company had so kindly paid.

By and large the school thing was pretty straight forward. We still laugh at the 'suitability' interviews we had to have. One in particular stands out, with the headmaster of Hall Grove School. We arrived in our posh Rolly Poly which we decided was a good start. He was a bit up himself and droned on a lot. He was very pleased to tell us how they all studied Classical Greek as part of the school's language programme. Like I would be impressed! I think the interview tanked when I replied that Ancient Greek would be very helpful when going to Greece on our next holiday. He wasn't impressed and needless to say, Ben wasn't accepted as we didn't meet their very high standards.

With our Ben it wasn't until he was sixteen, in his final year at Bearwood school, and had taken to drinking vodka that we had any problems. He was well liked and doing very well in classes. Following on from his shenanigans, and running around the school late at night, it was agreed that to complete his time at Bearwood, he should stay home and travel each day to school. I think that this was a nice way of firing him and still giving him the chance to finish the job.

It's funny but I often had reason to drive to work at 9am on a Saturday morning. I was driving along the same section of the motorway as Ben who, it turned out, was late again and on his way to school. I was cruising along at a steady, stay out of jail 85mph, when he comes flying past me in his black, boy wonder, birthday present Ford Escort. I just wonder where he got that from? Fair play though, and to everyone's surprise, Benjamin made us all proud coming out top of the school with a hangover and good grades in all his exams and qualifications. Not at all like me!

Claire was quite different and always very determined. Her first trip to hospital was aged two when, out shopping, she stood up in the buggy and fell out the back landing on her head. Aged seven, while on holiday in St Lucia, she ran through a huge plate glass window in the hotel bedroom. She was both very lucky and badly injured. She did wake up the next day in a Caribbean hospital. The only little white girl surrounded by lots of curious little black children. We had left her the night before when she was anaesthetised and out for the count. We had put in her cot a Sony Walkman and some books for when she woke up. When we arrived the next morning at 8am she was being so Claire. Completely engaged with all the other children who were reading the books and listening to her music. While learning to ski on a dry ski slope, she broke her hand. On another occasion she fell down the stairs and broke her leg. Claire and hospitals!

She was popular at school, smart and worked hard. The Marist was a good school with good teachers which is very important. A good teacher makes a connection and inspires their students to work hard, understand, and to do better. Claire was really good at her art and her art teacher did get the best

out of her as did Mrs Bates their gymnastics teacher. Over a few years, the school, along with Claire and her friends, won regional and national gymnastics championships. She has many medals and a much-coveted Blue Peter badge for appearing on national TV. We were all so proud of her.

I did have a problem when she was sixteen. The girls' senior school had appointed a man as its headmaster. Mr Richard, who it turns out, had a bit of as problem as a bully and liked to try it on with the senior girls. Claire was starting to struggle around that time. Like every bully, this head teacher sensed her vulnerability and liked to pick on her. One day it became a problem when she came home, very upset having had a nasty panic attack. It was brought on by this man singling her out in the middle of a crowd of girls, one afternoon for no apparent reason.

The next day I drove to the school at 9am and asked to see him. The secretary told me he was busy taking assembly, that I didn't have an appointment and he couldn't be interrupted. I wasn't in the mood for being nice and told her very clearly to go immediately and fetch him out or that I would go to assembly and get him out myself. It took a few minutes for him to appear. I had to shake him about a little, but the wormy little git quickly came to understand that if ever I had to come find him again… He never bothered Claire again.

Those family years just flew by. After Claire destroyed the hotel bedroom in St Lucia, we were welcomed back every year for a few years. The owners, Theo and Helen Gobat, were such lovely people and by way of consolation, gave us such a good family rate that we just couldn't stay away. The kids were always confident and polite. They weren't afraid to have a go and became adopted by the boat drivers, Bruno and Tony. The water sports guys were very fit and loved to do back flips and the like. They liked it even more when Claire would run along beside them and then do seriously impressive multiple flips and running somersaults. Thomas and Rebecca were still very young and loved spending every day with Kathy in the amazing kids club. For us, St Lucia was where we learned to windsurf, sail and water

ski. They would give Ben, one on one coaching since he proved to be such a good mono skier. For a few years those holidays were the best ever and we now added water sports trips as well as the snow skiing to our annual holidays.

With Patsie and Otto, Mike and Marylin, they both became our very good and dear friends. Along with their families, we did so much together and went together to so many places. Being a bit older than us they kind of showed us the way. In returning their hospitality we threw our share of big and sometimes crazy parties, both in the house and in the garden. We put on Christmas plays in the village hall and street parties in the street! We were so lucky that in my mum and dad, the children had such great grandparents. The children loved staying with them, and they loved having them. With such good babysitters we found ourselves living the life and we made sure we did. We went to concerts, opening nights at theatres, Henley, the Barclay Square balls, Royal Ascot, and Goodwood's big events. We had so many weekends away and some great times out. All with very good and special friends.

Before we knew it our babies, Ben and Claire, were driving, had their own cars and were off to their respective universities.

We encouraged them to be themselves and, since it didn't grow on trees, to work and earn what money they needed. We of course supported them by not making it too easy, but we were always around to help when and where it was needed. While at university, Claire and Rebecca turned out to be "our stars in waiting" working at Pizza Express and pocketing great tips. Ben, from the "School of Vodka", was better at making cocktails in Henry's or All Bar One.

In 1997 we all went on a Sunsail beach holiday where, for me, sailing boats played a big part. All the young'uns we met working there, were really lovely people, having fun and taking a time out. Instead of continuing the family tradition of working forever at Pizza Express we encouraged first Claire and then Rebecca and Ben, to go and do the same, have fun and work abroad. Initially for Sunsail in Greece and then ski chalets during the winter.

Wrong Place and Wrong Time

On 11th August 1999, the darkest and worst day of our life. I was working in the Oxford warehouse, and it was the day of the total eclipse of the sun. At 1pm there was an urgent phone call for me. It was Gail screaming down the phone. I will never get over that moment and that sound of her awful screams. In an instant, twenty-three years of our lives came crashing down. It took a while to get Gail to calm down and explain that Claire had been run over by a bus and killed.

No one but us will ever know how truly awful that moment was. We had both started out on our life together with nothing and had everything going for us. We loved, cared for, and protected the children that we had made. There was nothing else in our lives that really mattered, and, in an instant, Claire was unbelievably, forever gone.

Claire had been unwell and had taken a time out from university to get herself better. She and her then boyfriend Matt had been together for a couple of years. Claire was getting better and had organised herself to restart her studies at Brighton University that September. They were working their third summer, in Greece.

Matt was in the sail loft finishing a repair to a boat sail. Claire took the mini motorbike back to the shared staff house to get some money to buy ice creams. It was on the way back that the accident occurred. I cannot imagine how poor Matt had the courage to make that phone call to Gail on that day.

As soon as I had taken Gail's call, I knew what I must do. I had to take control, act quickly, and called our oldest son, Ben. There was no way or time, to sweeten this awful message. Poor Ben was only five minutes away from home, working down the road in a bar in Camberley. I needed him to go straight home. I was sixty miles away in Oxford and at twenty-four, he was my oldest. I trusted him to go straight home and get a hold of his mother and not let her go. Despite my being in shock and emotionally all over the place, it was clear in my head as to what had to be done.

I got back home to Camberley as fast as was possible. I was alone, driving on auto pilot, down a road that I had been commuting on for ten years. It was a horrible journey that I would never want to do again. I knew at 100mph a crash wouldn't help. I had to concentrate and stay focused as the reality of what had happened kicked in. The driving and concentration probably helped me get my head sorted giving me an hour to collect myself.

In a situation your brain works so fast. It's already worked out what you need to do as you mentally and slowly try to grind through your options. However much I hurt, I had to be the lead in the family, the one who tries to keep us all together. Slowly I came to realise what it was we had to do. My first priority was to get home safely and hold onto my wife, son, and daughter.

I called Rebecca who was halfway through a shift at Pizza Express in Bristol. I gave her some old story about her needing to come home immediately as her grandfather had been taken seriously ill. I don't think she believed me, but she did at least drive home straight away arriving about two hours later. Young Thomas was away on a school camping trip. We decided to leave him where he was keeping the terrible news until when he got home some days later.

In a situation like this, you have no choice other than to keep going, putting one foot in front of the other. We both knew we had to lead the way in support of what was now just Ben, Rebecca, and Thomas. We were struggling to function properly. I wanted to fly to Greece and just sit with our little girl, so that she wasn't alone. Gail sensibly helped and told me that it was more important to stay, and that I was needed more at home. Fortunately, the task of getting Claire home became very straightforward. We were all over the place and, thank goodness, our local undertakers were very professional. They quietly and simply took over the whole process.

Claire was flown back home to where we lived in three days. This was a big relief as it meant she was no longer a thousand miles away and all alone. We all set about helping her and getting everything ready for her final journey. We were a mess, but by now, all together and holding on. Having lots to organise and to do helped us to focus and it helped. We always knew we had smart, strong, and capable children. It was our love for Claire and each other that helped us keep it all together through this terrible period.

I had to read all the police reports. I made phone calls and talked and listened carefully to everything that was said. There was so much wrong with what happened on that day. The speed limit was 40kph and the bus driver admitted he was speeding. There was no tachograph record. Witness statements from the bus put him in the wrong. Even the conductor's statement said he was driving too fast, talking, and not concentrating on the driving. The accident took place on a straight country road with a 28mph speed limit. I couldn't see how this crash could possibly have ever happened. It was his carelessness and reckless driving that killed poor Claire.

I have always believed and told myself, that the driver, Nikolas Vlarkos, never left home that day intending to create such a horrible accident. However, it was his negligence and lack of care that took away the life of someone so young and who was so special to us.

Four months after the accident we went to the court hearing in Lefkas. Whilst it wasn't easy for us, we wanted to visit the scene of the accident. In the sunshine and after a shower we drove down the hill to Vasiliki, the village where Claire had worked and died. Within the last mile, as we approached there was a double rainbow stretching across the sky. It kind of felt like Claire was with us and somehow was trying to say something. At times like that it just wiped us out. She loved Christmas and so, for Claire, we had brought a Christmas reef, a decoration all the way from home. Using a rock, we nailed it to a nearby post, walked away and cried.

We went to the court, where the idiot solicitor we had employed, ranted, and raved. The court really weren't interested in him or what he had to say. Despite the many laws that were clearly broken and what happened to a young foreign seasonal worker, the driver was acquitted. As we left the courthouse the driver, a middle-aged man, was surrounded by his family, celebrating, smiling and all very happy.

We hurt so much and felt so completely useless. The court hearing was a joke and there was nothing else we could do. I had to drag poor Gail out and get her into the car and get away. I understood just how broken and hurt she felt. It was like we had let Claire down.

In the six hours it took, I don't think we spoke a word all the way back to Athens where we stayed overnight. The following day we drove back to the airport. Parking was difficult and no one seemed interested in helping us return the hire car. It was very busy, and I parked badly when some Greek bloke started laying into me, waving his arms around and shouting that I couldn't park there.

The bottled-up emotion, frustration and anger of the past few days just kicked in. It's the closet I have come in years to doing some serious injury to someone. My anger was such that I literally lifted this bloke off the ground by his jacket, shook him, shouted, and swore at him. He was terrified and I threw him down. I have no idea where he landed or why he had started on me. Wrong place and wrong time. I had more than had enough of the Greeks. The last I saw of him was with him pointing at me and telling some policemen about me. We left in a hurry, and I don't ever want to go back to Greece.

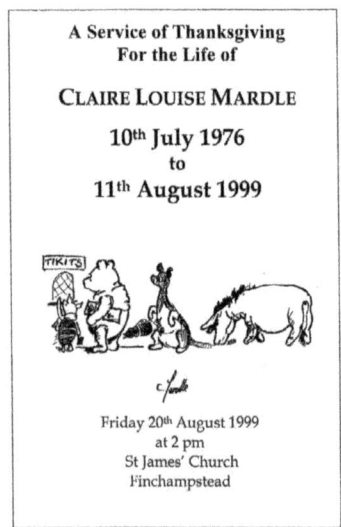

We will never forget the kindness shown by our friends and some of our family who were so good to us. The funeral was as beautifully done, as it should be, and we gave it our best shot. The little old country church at Finchampstead was decorated by us all, with flowers and candles and we knew Claire would have liked it. With Gail leading us in it felt really important that Ben, Rebecca, Thomas, and I carried Claire to the altar. The church was full of Claire's friends, her teachers as well as our friends and family.

I'm not sure how we got through any of this. At the time I didn't know how we could ever be normal again. How would we all carry on. We seemed to have bottled everything up and just didn't talk about it as a family. I have never felt able to discuss the accident and losing Claire with Ben, Thomas, or Rebecca. It was the same between Gail and me. We were each fighting our own battle and trying to ignore what had happened. Anytime we went anywhere near the subject it instantly brought everything back to the surface and we had to start all over again.

Ben looked after Claire when they were little. They had drifted apart during the university years. I still don't know to this day how our lovely, smart and kind big brother and son Ben managed or coped when in September, he went back to work, all on his own.

Rebecca and Claire had, however, become very close as big sister and little sister. It was only a few weeks earlier that Rebecca had been on holiday to see Claire in Greece, on her birthday and to spend time with her. I think and can understand how she took it all very badly. Like the rest of us she kept it to herself and somehow toughed it out. It messed her up for a couple of years though, again, we never talked about it.

Thomas was, I hope, a bit too young to take it all in. Perhaps it had helped his having been away at school for a few years and Claire being away at university and working abroad. This all meant that she wasn't around much for the six years leading up to the accident. He should, however, always remember how she called him "sweetie" read him stories and how he was always a much-loved little brother.

I so admire and respect how Gail handled herself and coped so bravely with this whole tragedy. After a month of our all being at home, we had to get back on with living. I employed people and after two weeks, had no choice other than to go back to work. This meant that Gail was so often left on her own and that must have been so hard. Although she was outwardly so strong, I know how much it broke her heart.

Thomas was fifteen and at boarding school. Ben was twenty-four, graduated, and setting out to start finding his own way in life. Rebecca was still at university with her then boyfriend who was massively supportive. We all kept very close, looking out for each other as we have always done. We all knew how much and how deeply this had hurt each of us. We all buried the pain and the unbelievable loss of our sister and daughter. It took a long while for each of us to recover our balance. We pushed the loss deep down while we each struggled to find our own way to work this out.

Instead of sitting around and dwelling on the situation, the five of us made a big effort and went to Thailand that Christmas. This also happened to be the big deal Millennium event. This trip was supposed to be special and to have included Claire. It was probably going to be the last time we all went away together as one family. Rightly, we stuck with the plan, smiled and we cried. We went riding around on elephants, smoked some big cigars and met some strange and confused blokes who honestly thought they were "ladies".

Somehow, we got through it as we "Mardles" always do.

Lots of well-intended people would dish out all sorts of old cliches meant to be encouraging. Most of them you instantly rejected, and some did help you to push on. I understood the importance of having to set goals, targets, and to find reasons to keep going and so that's what we did.

I knew I had to pick Gail up and help her find a reason to carry on. From year 2000 we immediately started to travel and to plan and then get on and do things. Gail and I went away and started travelling a lot. We went back to Spain where we bought a brand-new apartment which turned out to be the best thing we could have done. Both Rebecca and Gail went out there and got stuck in as it had to be finished and furnished.

Even now, after so many years, I can't describe the hurt and huge sense of loss that I know we all still feel. All along I believe it was all a terrible accident and that no one meant for this to happen. That mistakes were made, and that poor Claire paid the price. We have all buried 'our Claire' deep down in our hearts. She's still there, where we can each go in our own different ways and somehow, it's just best left there.

For me at quiet times or perhaps when driving home late at night, I can still imagine hearing her voice when I last spoke to her on the phone. If I close my eyes and drift, I can still feel her small hand holding mine when we were walking along the seafront road at Vounaki. It was Rebecca's eighteenth birthday and I bought them both stupid inflatable balloons from the street seller. We were all on our way to a crazy, never to be forgotten celebration dinner.

I last saw Claire, at bedtime, at the top of the stairs in our Tekels Park house.

**I clearly remember giving her a cuddle
and telling her to be careful out there.**

Mai Tais

Back in the twentieth century, you could buy an around the world, British Airways Club Class trip with seven stop overs, for let's say £1000. You had to travel in one continuous direction. In 1990 we chose to go west, west, and west. It was a while ago now and the numbers do get a bit blurred. We were young, doing very well for ourselves and in the prime of our lives. After all, you're not forty every year and so we found a way to afford this amazing once in a lifetime trip.

To kick off the celebrations, I threw a surprise fortieth birthday party for Gail at the five-star Complete Angler Hotel in Henley. This, thanks to Jim, my great father-in-law, was coincidentally the same venue as our wedding reception nineteen years earlier. I invited as many people as I could remember, or find, who had known Gail as she grew up. I suppose I had a chip on my shoulder. I never quite felt like I was an easy fit for the cliquey Buckinghamshire crowd. They all knew each other, had been to school together and hung out together. They seemed to be cruising along on the back of their fathers who had, post-war, successfully built businesses, and help put the town back on its feet.

That said, I seemed to get along with most of them and they

were never rude to me. By then I felt very good to be doing well enough on my own and in a position to bring them all together to our special celebration.

It was a party for Gail, and it was a chance for her to show off her lovely family. I think it made her feel good in that clearly, and against the odds, she had done all right in marrying outside the herd. I liked the idea that apart from me, the only other person to park a Rolls Royce outside the door that day was my father-in-law, Jim. A point that won't have gone un-noticed by him.

At the end of the reception, we bundled the kids into granny and grandpa's car, said our goodbyes and left for the airport. My parents were so good at letting us dump our family, whilst we selfishly went off on another trip. The only difference was that this time, it was to be a huge six weeks away.

Benjamin was fourteen and already at boarding school. For the six weeks away, we had arranged for eight-year-old Thomas to become a weekly boarder at Woodcote House, his prep school. He would get to come back and to join in the fun every weekend. Looking back, even if it did seem very selfish on our part, it all worked out and I would do it all over again.

We loved our children very much, and they loved being with their grandparents. The girls came and went on the school bus every day and Thomas came home at the weekends. My parents loved being a part of their growing up, had the energy and completely gave themselves over to the kids. They would all get one-on-one time, play games together and just hang out. I know they will never have forgotten those good times.

Unlike now, the BA lounge at Heathrow was very special in those days. The flight to San Francisco took twelve hours. We were picked up at LA International Airport by my long-time friend Rob Cavell and his NFL Soccer playing mate, Big Gerry.

It was Big G's car, and so he gave us the grand tour of San Francisco at 10pm that Sunday night. Gerry's specialty was copying the car chase from Steve McQueen's legendary movie,

Bullet, in his Ford Mustang. The only trouble was Jerry's car, the 'Gutless Cutlass' was no match for my all-time favourite car, the dark green, 365 Fastback Ford Mustang with black wheels. No matter, no one had told Gerry and we hurtled around the streets sliding all over the road. It was very much like you imagine being in a tumble dryer. We took off over all the humps and crashed down into all the dips. What an arrival.

We stayed with Rob, Lyndy and their dog PJ. Doing all the tourist stuff we thoroughly enjoyed being in America, me for my first time. We rented and drove a car from 'Rent a Wreck' to Sonoma in the Napa valley. A gorgeous lovely little town made of wood in the heart of the wine growing region. This turned out to be the delicious oaked chardonnay capital of the world. The red merlot wasn't bad either!

Hawaii was next but I wouldn't really recommend it to anyone. Being there you're supposed to like fast food and Dunkin Donuts. As a doughnut connoisseur, I can't see the point of drowning a perfectly good jam doughnut. The place is littered (good choice of word) with some ex-army Colonel's Fried Chicken as well as some Scottish clown's burger shops called McDonalds. The people in the hotels and bars drink Budweiser beer and go "Ye ha" a lot. The Margaritas were good and so was the departing flight.

Fiji's a great but small, rugby playing island in the middle of the Pacific Ocean. We were met and picked up by a genuine, and still in daily use, old 1950's coach-bus from Rosie's Tours. Rosie drove her bus, smoked marijuana, and drove us with great enthusiasm to the Regent Hotel. As we got off the bus, Rosie had a bad case of the munchies. Knowing that we had all just come from Hawaii, she asked each of us if we happened to have any old doughnuts.

The Regent turned out to be a lovely beachfront, wooden, five-star A-framed hotel, which was everything a Pacific Island hotel should be. It was at happy hour that we discovered Mai Tais, served every evening on the beachfront. This was when Fijian men in grass skirts looking like Maui, the demigod in Moana's film, came and lit the oil lamps to keep the evil spirits away. Not much of a worry there then. The Mai Tais already did that and as a bonus kept the mosquitos away as well. Once these blokes in the grass skirts had run along the beach and lit the lamps, they turned into an arrow-shaped line. Whipping out their balls they did the Fijian Haka, which finished drop kicking the balls into the sea as a warning to all and any sea monsters.

We met a lovely young couple of newlyweds on honeymoon from New Zealand (another great playing rugby nation). After a few sherbets, we felt like they probably needed someone to talk to. We must have looked safe and acted a bit like their parents. We told them about Mai Tais and its suitability as mosquito repellent. No pressure then and since they couldn't make up their minds what to order, we set about drinking all the cocktails on the menu. I rest my case. No one could remember getting bitten not even once!

Needless to say, it wasn't very long before we fell off the stools and couldn't stand up, let alone talk, but it was funny. The next day I went sailing with the bridegroom and a case of cold beers. It must have been the cocktails from the day before because we arrived back late, burnt and, once again, a little bit drunk.

Gail got along well with the new bride. The pair of them happily chilled for the day on sun beds sipping bottled water and eating cold watermelons. I do hope we didn't cause them to have a newlywed set to. I don't think we did since we all laughed a lot, and everyone seemed very happy! I wonder if they are still married or perhaps whether we contributed to their later in life dependency upon alcohol.

In Australia we stayed with Gail's sister Tina. We did all the sights and spent a lot of time hiding from all the giant Australian things that seemed to be determined to kill or eat you. We rented a car and drove around the Blue Mountains where it rained a lot. Not the same as English rain where you just get wet but biblical rain like what Noah floated his boat on.

The history books are clearly wrong about the great flood.

It's obviously written by some poor old middle slave trying to please a local oil prince like, Sheik Ur Willy. He had a bad habit of stoning his people to death or just chopping off their body parts after they had got themselves into trouble. It depended on what you had done as to what bit of you got chopped off. For stealing it was your hand. For telling fibs, your tongue, and weeing in the street, your willy.

This middle eastern top dog wanted a new image. A cock and bull story about a biblical, epic flood was needed to try and boost his tourism business. Firstly, the problem with being the top dog was that no one will ever tell you the truth. With this line of thinking there were obviously a few obstacles the get over. Firstly, it's a bloody great dessert and it never rains. Second there's no trees to build a boat and lastly there's no animals anywhere to be found let alone to put into the fictitious boat.

Fortunately, the real and true story was seen and remembered by the native Australian Abos. They are the ones who never bothered to write anything down. It rained and rained just like it still does in the Blue Mountains (they're not all blue). Once the Abo's god had pulled the plug out, all the water drained away as it does in Oz. The great ark was left high and dry on top of Ayers Rock. This was not very convenient although not too great a problem. It was all used afterwards to light up a great big Barbee. The animals, realising what goes onto the Barbee, all escaped, and it was a downhill jog and a race to get back to the beach for the survival party. This is also why there is nothing left to see at Ayers Rock so don't ever bother going.

Wherever we went, we always had fun and we stayed in some strange places. Our lasting impression, back then in 1990, was that Australia was like an English seaside town from the 1950s. It still had a long way to go to catch up.

The clock ticked away and before we knew it, we were waking up on another Qantas flight. It was bouncing around a lot and making lots of engine noises as we approached Hong

Kong airport. This was back in the day when the new airport was still being built and the Union Jack flew proudly over the old arrivals building. Like so many things of our old Empire, this airport, Hong Kong One, was built to take propeller planes.

Now, and many years on, we're on this big old Boeing 747 jumbo jet with four hundred passengers and a lovely upstairs Club Class cabin. It's worth remembering that back in those days the upstairs of a jumbo was a very special "Club" room. The club lounge had enough space for tea dancing to the quartet. It was where people dressed for dinner and the casino stayed open to very late.

While all this was going on you had to give full marks to the brave pilots, both of whom had probably flown Lancaster bombers during the war. As you approached HK you could look out of one window to see we were flying between mountain peaks. The next minute, looking out of the other window, the aeroplane was tilting downwards looking at sampans and Chinese junks and what they were having for breakfast. I'm pragmatic and these flying jockeys must have done this loads of times. They know the difference between Singapore and Hong Kong One, right?

I am not making this up. The next thing we see, out of the window, is we are flying down the middle of the badly named 'High Street'. Shops are everywhere, on either side, all with loads of people and flashing neon signs. This huge giant of an aeroplane, wheels down, flaps extended, and engines roaring is flying just above the third-floor rooftops of restaurants and homes. You can tell they are restaurants because they're all painted on the roof for the benefit of passing planes: "Lovely Jubbly Food and Valet Parking." Who, I ask you, and how and where can you park a bloody great jumbo jet?

This is the craziest airport I have ever landed at. In fact, I can't believe it's even allowed. We're flying so low, right down the middle of the very busy shopping street. Now I'm worried,

so what would have happened if the traffic lights had changed?

We stayed at the fabulous, no expense spared, Amari five-star hotel. Hong Kong has plenty of those. They have so many people doing everything for you which makes going to the men's toilet a real worry. No sooner have you gone in then a little man comes rushing over waving a wet wipe, pulls your zipper down and wants to point Percy at the porcelain for you. Enough I say! Being shown to our room and coming out of the lift there was even a man there, making little sandcastles on the top of the rubbish bins just for your pleasure.

Remember, we had never done anything like this or been anywhere as different, it was amazing. Hong Kong has crazy old trams, famous ferry boats, glitz, wealth, and fantastic shops where you can buy ground-breaking electronics.

We were thinking that after six weeks away the children would probably never talk to us again. To head off our feelings of guilt and to try and win back their love and affection, we bought stuff. Nintendo, Super Mario handheld electronic games. Gameboys, handheld personal gaming devices (Tetras). Two player games consoles that had fifty built-in video games. This was 1990! And remember this stuff still hadn't been invented. It was all so amazingly good.

We caught a train to China for two nights, at a time when western people didn't go to China. Gail was the blue-eyed fashionista from the west. I was the six-foot tall, bearded giant in jeans. We so didn't fit in with the thousands and thousands of people, all on bicycles. They would all stop and stare at us in an inquisitive but polite way. There were lots of lorries and mopeds but not many cars. As you travelled around you saw thousands of ducks from Peking as well as sweet and sour pigs, all happily wallowing around in muddy ponds. In China, ducks and pigs were everyone's all year-round favourite and about as lucky as English turkeys at Christmas. We caught a boat out into Aberdeen harbour for dinner at the famous Jumbo Floating Palace. Guess what dinner was, hmmm, Peking duck and sweet and sour pork.

All the time there we had to have a guide. We were only allowed to go out accompanied and even then, only to where we were told to go. There were lots of uniformed officials and police keeping everything in order. Some things like a visit to a school were put on just for us to see. I think it's now a very different place these days. People talk about how China has 1.2 billion people and is very crowded. What we can tell you is that they are all half size and only take up the room of 600 million and so far less of a problem.

Our seventh and final stop off on our 'round the world ticket' took us to India's centre of government, New Delhi, arriving at four thirty in the morning. We cleared immigration and wandered out to try to find our transport. It was probably the scariest place we had ever found ourselves in. All around and everywhere we went there were just so many Indians. Hardly surprising since we were in the heart of a country of one billion people.

It was dark and cold. There were soldiers everywhere in old Second World War greatcoats with Lee Enfield rifles slung across their shoulders. The time of day didn't matter. Despite this being the international airport, there were snake charmers and people everywhere cooking on open fires. People were just curled up sleeping on the floor and it didn't smell very nice.

I had to leave the building to go find our driver. I left Gail inside the arrivals hall thinking the scary soldiers would look after her. She would be all right so long as she kept away from the snake charmer. I finally found our man asleep in his car with a sign on the window that said 'Mardles do not disturb'. What a cheek, so I woke him up and off he stumbled away to the toilet. Eventually we all set off to the Meridian hotel.

Once we had slept for a bit, we decided we had no time to lose. This was, after all, to be the last stop on our amazing journey. We needed to go see as much as we could. It was like we had landed on another planet. The view from our tenth-floor room across Delhi was amazing. We stepped out of the hotel to discover a world of mopeds, bicycles, cows and of course the Tuk-Tuks, for the very first time. We tripped over some people just sleeping, stepped around some beggars, and headed for the cleanest looking Tuk-Tuk. A relief then to find everyone wobbles their heads at a question and speaks very good English. We asked how much for a tour of New Delhi. Joginder, that was his name, said no problem. That we should just pay him what we thought it was worth, at the end. We didn't know any better, and Joginder knew he had lucked in that day.

We hammered straight around to the petrol station. Jogi asked for a sub of five hundred rupees to fill up with. I say we hammered around but really this was just what it is like being in a Tuk-Tuk for the very first time. It's a Lambretta scooter only with three wheels and a covered pram like back. It drives at 15mph, and it shakes and the engine sounds like it's being hammered by a hundred little hammers, all the time. The scary bit is finding out that we're sitting on top of the fuel tank and that everything and anything is red hot.

What a great city with fabulous buildings, historical forts, buildings and temples. We took great care and were prepared for the poverty as well as all the begging. It's still quite shocking and a lot to take in. However, despite everyone wearing flip flops, most people come across as being busy, working hard and above all else, happy.

Joginder drove us around in the Tuk-Tuk food blender for two hours, pointing out and telling us lots about this fabulous city. Finally, on our first day, dropping us back to our hotel and

the moment of reckoning. Gail and I looked at each other and said to him we have no idea. He of course just wobbled his head and said, "How much it had been his pleasure." It was no matter and just to pay whatever we felt it was worth. I think we bunged him a pony (£25) which we now know, translates to a month's wages in India.

Everyone likes a piece of the pie and the hotel sensibly suggested we use a guided tour for the rest of our journey. This company would of course have been the managers brothers. A Mr Singh arrived the next day in an old English Austin Ambassador car circa 1960. He was a very well-educated Sikh university teacher prejudicially forced out of his job by the ruling Hindu party. A lovely gentle man who treated us like royalty. He told us so much of the history and showed us all the amazing places around Delhi. It was probably him, and his car, which made us so want to come back one day.

In-Competent Crew

It's 1994 and my son Benjamin and I had been on a competent crew sailing course for a weekend on the Solent. I had been going to night school learning about boats, tides, and chart reading. We had both cracked windsurfing and dinghy sailing while on holidays. I, of course, had benefitted from sailing single handed from Greece to Albania whilst on a holiday. A subscription to *Practical Boat Owner* which was always extremely helpful in telling you how to sail safely in a hurricane. We felt we were ready to take the next step, so what could be the problem.

Unlike me, my brother John who has a really useful box of spanners, is much better at anything with an engine. He helped by being technical when we bought our first boat from a company in Southampton. It was a classic, pretty little boat, twenty-seven feet long with a double cabin, a toilet that you had to manually pump and a kitchen galley. The toilet was interesting as well as funny. Having done your business you shut the lid, pumped like crazy and fired the unwanted bits out the bottom of the boat. Once they had banked our cheque, they very helpfully chucked it into the water for us.

Looking back, I have so often thought, was I really a very

responsible father? On so many occasions, I think, I might have got it wrong. Like teaching Ben to drive aged four sitting on my lap and driving my work's Ford Cortina down French country roads on the way to the baker to get the croissants. All I can say is that, thanks to me, he did pass his driving test first time.

Well, on the big day, the second-hand boat salesman didn't hang around for long. He and his team briefly lined up on the quay and, with a waiting customer who wanted to buy a 70ft super yacht, waved us both bon voyage. Ben, aged fourteen, and I decided as it was 3pm we had better put the time spent at the night school to effective use. We did a tide look up calculation. We sniffed the wind. Set a pencil plan across the map and worked out where and how we were going to get to Chichester. By the time we had found the sails, started the engine, and let go of the ropes, it was 4pm.

Importantly though, with lots of people looking on, we thought we looked good. Ben was dressed like a Formula One mechanic, and I was dressed for wet weather gardening.

At night school they tell you to plot your course at the average rate of 5mph. What we now discovered is that the strong tides in the Solent can run against you at 6mph. That the wind never is in the right place, and everything conspires to just slow you down or even go backwards! Against the tide, even if you have the sails up and the engine on you make terribly slow progress. Well, no matter, we are very conscientious and did what the teacher had said. We marked our chart every half hour. Kept a good look out for crazy people playing cricket on the bramble bank, wind surfers, pedalos and cruise ships. In fact, we did everything it says in the book.

It was 6pm and in three hours, we had eaten all the biscuits and had only gone halfway. We had reached Portsmouth, home of the Royal Navy, and it was beginning to get dark. There were flashing lights everywhere. It tells you on the sailing chart what and where they are. In the *Sailing for Dummies* book, they say some you go around and some you just go past. Some are on the left, and some are on the right. Some are just for your information, and you're not supposed to crash into them. Some on the other hand, are just outside the fish and chip shop in Gosport high street. By now you are overwhelmed, very confused and thinking fish and chips would be good.

We weren't going into Portsmouth harbour on this occasion and so all we had to do was avoid all the Saturday sailors, the hovercrafts, the aircraft carriers, submarines, and cross channel ferries. It's like having just passed your driving test and driving through central London for the very first time. We were feeling exceedingly small and quite out of place.

By now it was dark, and we had to find the switch to put our navigation lights on. Previously we had been able to see the Isle of Wight, Portsmouth, and even where we were going. Chichester was still eight miles away and in the dark, we couldn't see it. It was time to man up and to start acting like real sailors using the compass and the chart.

Having a smart youngster along was clearly the right thing to do. He reads the chart and tells me what colour flashing lights we should be looking to find and in which direction we should be going. By 8pm it's cold and we think we have found the Chichester tower. It's sticking up, way out in the water marking the 'dangerous entrance' to the harbour.

No one told us that the entrance was a bit tricky. It's a half-mile wild roller coaster of wind, waves, and a big sea. It's better suited to surfing, rather than sailing. Once in it you are kind of stuck with it and there's no turning back. We know it's dark and, against the background of the land, we can see where we need to go. We thought it can't be that hard as loads of people do it. After all, we're Mardles and no matter what happens, we know we usually come out all right. I hugged my son, told him I loved him, and we put on the lifejackets, got our torches ready and went for it.

Once out of the tumble dryer, that's the approach to the harbour, we arrived in the calm stretch of water leading into the great big natural harbour. Again, we found ourselves surrounded by more flashing lights. Now, if you've never done this before, believe me it's very difficult. It's cold, dark and getting late. You're in the middle of the water and it's big and dark either side on the riverbanks. You have a chart which says to stay in the middle of the channel or run aground and sink. Like joining up the dots, you must go from one light to another. There are red ones, green ones, white ones, and even yellow ones. Some flash at different rates and some don't flash at all. We both continue peering into the darkness and looking at the chart. Then, after another mile, amongst all the clutter and lights we are told we must find a single green light, flashing twice, every five seconds.

Assuming you've got that right we then had to turn left down an even darker river towards Bosham, our final destination. Well, we finally got there and after shining our torches all over the place, we eventually tied up our new, first boat. We were well and truly exhausted, but rightly very pleased with what we had achieved on our first boating adventure.

We spent fifteen years mucking about and getting cold and wet on England's south coast. It wasn't as hard as people think. You read all the sailing magazines which would have you believe it was all doom, gloom, and hurricanes. The reality was that with common sense, patience, and Fisherman's Friends, you gradually work things out, slowly getting better at the business of sailing. When it went wrong, which it often did, then you just had to deal with it, stay calm and learn from your mistakes.

I did a lot of sailing with my brother and friends on a lot of different boats. It was always cold sailing in the Solent during the spring and autumn. In summer when it was nice, there was never enough wind. To be a sailor in England, you must be a certain type of person. Quite tough, adaptable, and always wearing a hat. I'm sure sailing is really a bit like caravanning. Everyone is very 'jolly' and loves to chat. However, unless your caravan/boat is of a decent size and with all the bits, fridge, freezer, microwave, toilet, and of course with a hot shower, then you just have to make do.

That means when you want a shower or a poo it's best to go ashore and use 'the facilities'. The marina washrooms were never warm and always awash. Drop your trousers, take off your clothes and even with great care, they always got wet. Still, the hot water and the shower made you feel both clean and normal again. I have to say I never felt right shaving and brushing my teeth in a line with other men. I think perhaps it was a bit like being in prison.

Once back on board the coffee's never that great and without a fridge, you drink red wine since the white wine, like the beer, is always best served chilled. Cooking on little boats was never easy. Sailing with the boys, it was always a Full English whereas when on your own, you just end up eating disgusting food like cornflakes, or boiling pasta smothered in jars of 'Mamma's Pasta Sauce'.

The thing is, with sailing it's always about the starting and the finishing. You get all kitted up and have plenty to do at both ends of the journey. Once on the way, you get to stand on the front of the boat with a rope in your hand looking like you're heading off on a dangerous adventure. That's when you feel like a 'super cool pro' whilst the 'grockles' enviously look on. Grockles, I learned, are the people who just hang around harbours and seafronts eating ice creams, walking their overweight dogs and just watching.

I think we always had a regard for staying safe and I don't remember ever feeling afraid. We quickly learned that the first boat was really not that good. It sailed badly, was too small, and it leaked a lot. It relied upon a silly lawnmower-type engine which was hidden in a cupboard. It was a pig to start and always stopped at the most critical moments.

On one occasion John and I sailed to Brighton for a drink. Once in the harbour we needed to top up the water tank. Off we went for a bevvy or two but forgot to turn off the hose before we left. When we returned hours later the inside of the boat was half full of water and it was visibly sinking. I honestly don't think the boat ever properly dried out after that.

At another time we were sailing around in the dark and lost track of the time as well as the Bacardi. We then missed our table reservation in Port Solent where we planned to stay for the night. Even if late, the manager was delighted to have what I think he believed was a part of a Formula One team in his bar. I don't think he quite understood that John and Gordon weren't actually the drivers. He was happy, took lots of photos and he even let Gordon make the cocktails behind the bar for the next few hours.

When we left at two in the morning doing the Bacardi waltz: that's one step to the side, two steps forward, one step sideways and finishing with one more step but backwards. I never could dance and slipped down the wall and fell into the harbour. Gordon just lay down and fell asleep on the bench and no one ever saw or cared where John had gone.

It wasn't always funny. One Sunday, John ended up in hospital when I wasn't paying attention. The mainsail suddenly flipped from one side of the boat to the other. The ropes and big main sail flattened and crushed him. It was very scary, and he ended up in Chichester hospital.

The point was that boats can be dangerous as well as a lot of fun! It had however shown me the way and I had had so many unforgettable moments in those early years.

Come Fly With Me

It was 2010 and I had read about Wilbur Wright and the first powered flight which had taken place at Farnborough near to where we lived. It was truly inspirational, so my youngest son, Thomas, and I decided we needed to get into this flying stuff. We booked and turned up at Booker airfield near High Wycombe for our first gliding experience. They told us we wouldn't be allowed to just go out on our own. That to begin with we had to take a step back and, like children learning to walk, going up in the air on reins and without an engine.

Upon reflection we thought they probably knew what was best. We were asked to change into Tom Cruise look-alike jumpsuits and to put on the slim one-size-fits-all parachutes. Now, I've always had a problem with this one-size-fits-all malarky. Thomas, who hasn't lived as long or as well as me, is still slim, fit, and young. He really did look the part in his Top Gun clothing and the neat and tidy escape parachute. I, on the other hand, look like a badly fitting and oversized beanbag with a broken zip.

In a worst-case scenario and we fell out of the glider, Thomas at 50 kilos would float around enjoying the view for ages. Like all

young'uns he's never parted from his phone. He would probably get some really good pictures of Berkshire and the glider crashing, before landing gently on the ground. I'm worried now since at 100 kilos the science says, using the same lightweight, compact parachute, I will drop out of the sky twice as fast as Thomas. In the short time it would take to hit the ground I would still not have gotten the phone out of my pocket, let alone take any bloody pictures. With my luck I would have landed on some soft fir trees, bounced safely into a pond, and then had the empty aeroplane come crashing down on top of me.

Our new friend the instructor, who introduced himself as Gerry-Onimo, told us not to worry. It's all quite normal and that what goes up always comes down. The ground crew, all spectacularly dressed in tight clinging latex suits, walked us across to the hangar where they kept the little beasties. Now, bear in mind this is the discounted trial first lesson and that they want you to come back. They are putting on a show for you. As they opened the hangar doors the theme music from *Top Gun* blared out and the strobe lighting flashed and sparked.

They rolled the beautiful, shining little white glider out into the beautiful sunshine and onto the strip.

Thomas and I drew straws for who would go first. I got the short one and climbed in squashing my all-important nuts, and now even more compact, parachute. The loud music faded away and the psychedelic lights were turned off. Gerry-Onimo, being no fool, put me in the front seat. I guess I was to be the air bag in the event of anything going wrong before we left the ground. The ground boys then pulled all the safety straps tight; my voice went up several octaves, and they went round checking all the knobs and levers.

The tension was building, and my nerves were all wobbling at the same time. To get us away, they went and fetched an old, leftover, First World War aeroplane with a very long tow rope. The bloke flying this antique was called Jolly Johnnie. He just sat there, quietly smoking his pipe, waiting for us to get it all sorted out. They clipped the two aeroplanes together using the rope. I then understood and was disappointed that there was to be no steam catapult. Humph, they would use one if you were Tom Cruise or on an aircraft carrier. I confess I was a little disappointed but for the money we paid it was OK.

The ground crew, in their Toys'R'Us Spandex costumes, went professionally about the business of closing the big Perspex cockpit canopy. They kept shouting to each other things like 10:4

and 2:2 as well as and making cool hand signals while waving tennis bats around. Gerry-Onimo was in radio touch with Jolly Johnnie, he being the other pilot in the tow plane. He did a few hand signals and stuck his middle finger up to the ground crew who were waving both their arms up and down as if they were birds flying.

Gerry-Onimo shouted to me above all the noise, to hang on and not to touch anything. That the pull lever would open the cockpit canopy in the event of an emergency. We would then be finding ourselves sky diving at no additional cost. There would be no inflight service on this journey today the use of mobile phones was strictly unnecessary. With a jerk the two connected aeroplanes started to move forwards across the grass strip and down towards the end of the airfield. The radio crackled as we lined up getting ready to go. Gerry-Onimo and the fat controller up in the control room waffled on. They were doing the '10:4, 2:2, wind 320 west and twelve knots foxtrot uniform and Bob's your uncle and you're clear to go', routine.

With a great big lurch and lots more engine noise we were off. Before you can get up into the air, tradition says you have to get dragged all over the field. It's like sitting on a tea tray, being pulled along by a demented lunatic, all the while being shaken to pieces. The 100-year-old bi-plane in front swerves left and right. Worryingly as the speed increases, the wheels keep leaving the ground as it bounces up and down. I'm worried about the bit of string that connects us as the little glider swerves around madly.

There's a big hedge at the end of the strip and Johnnie, in the mother ship, sensibly lifts up off the ground to avoid hitting it. We, on the other hand, are seventy-five feet behind it and I now realise why I'm sitting in the front. I can only hope Gerry-Onimo is paying attention. He was and blow me if we didn't take off as well. We are now flying and I'm thinking Neal Armstrong, and this was another first step for mankind, me, and my family.

It was three or four minutes of flying up and up, in tandem and behind the tow plane. Gerry shouts across that we're going to "let go the tow". He has two levers, one for the canopy, which he had warned me not to touch, and one to release the tow cable. What can I do other than to trust him, and he easily and smoothly drops the Halfords-special tow rope. The noise had suddenly all gone. We were silently turning away from the now long-gone tow plane which was heading home ready for the next and completely bonkers launch.

We swooped and soared, we had dived down for more speed and rose up on the thermals. The only noise was the wind across the wings and the clonk as we clobbered some of England's few remaining sparrows. It was a super view from two and three-thousand feet. What comes across is the amount of pure countryside and how many trees there are within a short distance of some grubby little town. Gerry-Onimo bravely gives you control and instructs on how turn, what to go looking for and how to find your way back to the airport. This, he said, was quite important as landing on the M40, with no wheels, could be a bit messy.

With this in mind we had to go about landing. I thought taking off was bad enough. Landing was even worse since we didn't have Jolly Johnnie and his antique aeroplane to help. We did a few three-sixty turns while descending to five hundred feet. Gerry-Onimo then takes his hands off the control stick, puts on his reading glasses, and reads the required airline landing regs from a card. Please put your trays in the upright position, stop being blind and return your seats to the upright position?

Once done, while still wearing his reading glasses, he worryingly asks me to point to the airport so he can line us up with the landing strip. From quite a long way out we start the approach. Then suddenly, like a roller coaster at Thorpe Park, he points the nose of the glider straight down at the ground and yells out a "Ye ha". Clearly this is his favourite bit although I am so not sure if this is all good. He's got us pointing very aggressively at the ground and there's another big hedge at the other end of the airstrip. At the very last minute he shouts, "Whoa," like he's talking to a horse. He pulls back on the driving stick making the front of the glider point up towards the sky. We then touch down on the grass ever so gently and start all over with the tea tray routine. Were completely out of control, rushing along the ground at fifty miles an hour until running out of energy just in front of the hangar.

Of course, as the dad, I have to put on a brave face and a big smile as it's now Thomas's turn to have a go. They opened the Perspex canopy and pop all the straps telling me to get out. Jolly Johnnie is sitting in his aeroplane still smoking his pipe, watching. My voice had gone back down to normal, and my heart rate had seriously gone up. Being all lightheaded, I tripped and fell over the parachute straps while getting out and landed flat on my face. Now I have a lot more respect for Wilbur Wright.

Gail wasn't impressed!

Seniors Backpacking

The young'uns like to go on a pilgrimage once they find out that instead of getting a job, they can take another year off. They call it a gap year. When they come back, they tell us about the amazing adventures and places they have ended up going to. How they stayed in basic but exotic beach huts for ten dollars a night and bungee jumped into the middle of the Earth while looking for hobbits. How they got to feed the killer sharks and hunt for the great white whale, Moby Dick. We were envious and thought, if they could all do it then it can't be that hard. Why should they have all the fun? As ambassadors on behalf of all fifty-year-olds, we would take up the challenge and do the same. We set ourselves a target of fifty dollars a day and in 2003 booked flights to Singapore, Australia, and New Zealand.

The trip was booked, and the taxi was set to arrive at 08am to take us to Heathrow. I leaped out of bed (not true). Did a few push ups and opened the curtains (we didn't have any) and with no clothes on, frightened all the rabbits. There was snow everywhere. Not just the normal sprinkling but the biblical stuff like you see in one of those end-of-the-world disaster movies. Mohammed, the taxi driver, didn't show up, saying he was cold and had never seen snow before, let alone driven in it. This then was a problem. All the people trying to get to work and doing the school run, had chosen to get their Ford Fiestas out. They then decided to drive into each other's front gardens, parked cars, as well as each other. We were left without a choice if we were to get away. We stuffed the cases into Gail's Porsche as best we could and joined in the madness. It was still snowing, and we had no survival equipment, no hot drinks, and no shovel. After half an hour we had gone half a mile and knew we were never going to make the flight.

While sitting in the car, I phoned the insurance company and told them that the taxi had not arrived. They said, "Ha ha, you're not covered unless the car you were travelling in had broken down." OK, make them happy. So, we hung up and called them back telling them the car had broken down. They were very good and the following day we were on our way to Singapore via Koh Samui Island in Thailand.

On our budget of fifty dollars a night, like good backpackers, I booked an on-the-beach yoga retreat for a week. I thought Gail would like this and that she would be happy. It turned out she wasn't impressed as it was worse than awful, and she wasn't happy. We checked out in the morning before we came down with Ebola or something worse. As my luck would have it, and after this moment of unhappiness, we went OB (over budget) and went to stay in a lovely five-star beachfront hotel for the rest of the week. Gail was very happy.

After Koh Samui, we restarted our backpacking trip. We were trying to blend in as backpackers when we rocked up at Raffles, the most famous hotel in Singapore. It was Gail's birthday and I had always wanted to stay there. The taxi driver dropped us away from the front door and left us to drag our compact, soft travel bags up to the front door. The porters weren't very impressed and didn't try to help us to reception.

That all changed once they realised, I was a British Airways captain, staying on a BA staff rate. We were whisked up to our suite where we met our butler, who had made Gail a birthday cake, and wanted to polish our trainers? Raffles was old, colonial and very pretty with lovely 800-thread cotton sheets and pillowcases.

As backpacking ambassadors and being on a strict budget! we had to get back on track and soon found ourselves landing in Brisbane, Australia. We took the backpackers' shuttle bus along with six other young people, to a hostel. It was great. For ten bucks they gave us a little shoe bag like you first got in primary school. In it you had your cup, plate, knife, fork, and spoon as well as a room key. It was clean, bright and had a pointless and huge jacuzzi bath. You put your food in the communal fridge, having written your name on it. All the young people we met were amused but respectful, helpful, and so very nice. I guess we reminded them of their sponsors back home.

The following day, using an A4 tourist map of Australia, we caught the bus for what turned out to be a 300-mile road trip to a place called Mayborough. In reality it was a long way although it hadn't looked so far on the little A4 map! The front of the bus was protected by great big kangaroo bars and a super tough mesh screen. These were necessary to stop the flying stuff from breaking through the windscreen, killing the driver, and then eating all of us passengers.

We travelled through the day and night stopping frequently to pick up and drop off passengers. The stop offs were usually in some quaint old wooden frontier towns with bus stops in the middle of the town squares. Upon arrival, the guys at the bus station dropped the 'fly' screen and pressure washed all the bodies off. Some were the size of your hand. Nothing in Australia is small or friendly and everything seems to be out to kill you. The driver told us we were lucky this time out. There were no dead kangaroos or the local indigenous Abo's to extract from the 'Roo Bars'.

Using our fifty dollars a day backpacking budget, we squashed ourselves into took the minibus and onto to the next hostel. That evening we went out into what was like being in

Jurassic Park. We sat on a bench for an hour watching thousands upon thousands of huge bats taking to the sky at sunset. During the day they just hang around, upside down, in the trees. It turns out that every evening they just kept on coming, tracking across the ski from left to right, in search of baby Koala Bears to eat.

The following morning, we had booked ourselves onto an OB 'bush baby flight' to a wild and deserted place called Fraser Island. They put Gail and both our bags onto one side of the plane along with the pilot. Then they somewhat rudely put me, without cases, on the other side to try and balance the weight out. The flight was like being fired from a catapult. Loads of noise and action had us up into the air and before we knew it heading nose first down towards the island, landing on the beach running parallel along the very edge of the sea.

We were given a lecture about how to survive on our own. Basically, they said to stay in the truck that they gave us. If you did get out, then don't touch anything. Try not to go to the toilet in the bush and do stay away from the wild dingo's. They called the pickup truck a 'Ute'. It came fully equipped with a tent, sleeping bags, a cooking pot, and a torch. They told us to go anti-clockwise around the island and to stay on the track, which we did. This then was real time outback boy scout adventure as we bounced  along in our Ute, carefully watching out for danger. Very slowly we drove along until we came to a beach where we decided to make camp. No sooner had we put the tent up, then the savage, man, woman and childeating dingo's started circling. I was once in the 52nd Epping Forest Boy Scouts and so setting up camp and lighting a fire was straight forward. I also got badges for cooking and boiled up a superb Boy Scout-pasta for dinner. We had our eye on the doggies as well as leaving the doors of the Ute open just in case we had to get in quickly.

We survived the night taking it in turns to listen out for the wild beasts. Eventually they sent the baby bush aeroplane back for us. We handed over the Ute and flew back to the mainland bus stop for another epic 300-mile drive to our next destination, Airlie Beach.

It was there that they have the legendary Hog's Breath Café. I'm not criticising Australia for being backwards but I can tell you that it took eighteen hours to cook a steak in that restaurant. If you ever choose to go there, then you really need to get there and to place your steak order early. It's lovely to think that it's now owned by Matt, the husband of Sasha Bletzer, daughter of our dear friends Patsie and Otto.

It was from here that we took an OB yacht charter going off to sail around the southern end of the Great Barrier Reef. Before the bloke would let us take the boat, he insisted watching me drive it around the harbour. Happy then that I could sail? He rented us the $100,000 bit of kit.

Remember this is Australia and everything that lives there is out to get you! We were given what's called stinger suits to wear when we went into the water. The story goes that, at this

time of the year, there's a likely chance of your being attacked by angry, Australian, jellyfish. If they find out you're an English pom, they will try and sting you. Then you stand a very good chance of having a heart attack and dying. They were an optional thirty Ozzy dollars rental. So instead of dying we had to have them and to try them on for size. They were like giant black body bags, which they probably were. Once again and not for the first time, we looked like such a pair of plonkers.

We sailed to some lovely places anchoring, which is the way I like it, all on our own under the stars. We sailed around the Whitsunday Islands and visited the exclusive, wealthy, and famous Hamilton Island for lunch. We dinghied ashore to walk along some beautiful beaches, White Haven Beach being one of the most spectacular in the world. It's miles of pure coral white sand. No people and a beautiful tropical backdrop of trees and rivers.

We eventually left Australia and flew to Christchurch, New Zealand late in the day. Still trying to be good backpackers! we took the Trans Alpine train across the mountains to a place called Greymouth. The views from the glass observation car were fabulous as we crossed the mountains from one side of the island to the other. The mountain stops, the stations and signals were straight out of the 1950s which is, in part, how the whole of New Zealand is.

Once on the other side of the South Island, and being on budget, we took another bus only this time to see the glaciers at Franz Josef where we hoped to find a woolly mammoth. I know I keep banging on about the budget, but we only intended to do this the once. So, going OB again, we flew by helicopter to the very top of the glaciers and then went for a nice walk on the ice.

When it came to leaving, we naturally enquired about the next bus. It turned out they only ran every three days and never on Sundays. That was very annoying as we were time limited The

next bus wasn't for another two days. OK, so nothing else for it, we would hitch hike. I, of course, had done it all over Europe and many times before.

Gail will tell you, hanging out with me was never dull for long.

After two hours my thumb was beginning to feel tired. When ten or twenty cars had gone past, some lovely man stopped and offered us a lift. He turned out to be a taxi driver trying out his

new car. He wouldn't take any money and insisted on acting as our tour guide for the next five hours. He would stop the car and take us up some trail to see the most amazing sites. With typical NZ hospitality he even went and found us a place to stay once we had reached Queenstown.

If you've never been white water rafting, you're forty or under, I recommend you give it a go. The drive from our hostel up into the mountains was scarier than the rafting itself. The track was only wide enough for a fat donkey and not for a minibus stuffed with six people. Looking out the passenger window the drop was 500 feet straight down the side of the mountain. It was so narrow you couldn't see the edges of the road. It was very clever since you were so relieved to arrive without dying, the next part of the day was a doddle.

To begin with they put you in a wetsuit and a lifejacket and chuck you into the freezing cold mountain water. If you get out OK, and can still breathe and talk, they give the thumbs up and tell you to get into their giant inflatable raft. Once in they make it very clear that you will get wet, and that you will probably fall in. Instructions will be shouted at you. It's all about when to paddle and when not to. They tell you at other times, when they're not yelling at anyone, to just let the expert oarsman steer.

His job is to try not to get us all killed. Seriously this is big league Alton Towers and it's a blast.

So as to not waste the opportunity we flew in a small plane over the spectacular fjords and waterfalls. In NZ you can't help but to enjoy the locally produced food and wine. Things really do taste better and the Vino is legendary. We became convinced that the Kiwis were not daft. Keeping the best wines for local consumption and shipping the rest to France. We met a 1950's vintage car rally shipped all the way from England. During our time there we had seen fabulous sunrises and sunsets. Some spectacular scenery and never once a hobbit, dwarf, or a troll.

Wellington, the Kiwi capital, was on the North Island. NZ is a surprisingly big place considering the overall population is only 5 million people. To get there we had to fly from the south island. Always trying for the backpackers' hostel and back to our daily fifty dollars meant staying on the edge of town. For something to do we signed up to go sailing on a great big old square rigged sailing ship. It was the Admiral's Cup sailing race, and we were to be the downwind marker boat. That meant all the state-of-the-art yachts had to sail around us. It was very spectacular and won by the Swiss boat (all crewed by New Zealanders). In the end it was a shame to be leaving New Zealand, a campervans paradise. The people are lovely, and it really is a step back in time. In terms of simple pleasures, it's one of the loveliest places we have been. It's a long way away from England and if you get the chance just go there once.

My Dad Knew Nelson

Around 2004 I had sold my second boat down at Southampton. I got fed up with being cold, wet, and never having enough wind to make the blinking thing move. I had known for a long time that, aged fifty-four, I wanted to do something really different. I had this idea that you could give up the day job and just sail away.

The kids were seriously grown up and we were still able. It would be so different to what we had been doing for the past thirty years. We would have to be brave, out of our comfort zone and to be challenged. I know I'm not very good at fixing things, but I am good at making do. I have had a lot of sailing experience both on my own and with friends. Since lots of people do it, what could be so hard? We would sail the Caribbean going from island to island. It's exotic, English speaking, warm and with lovely steady weather (outside of the hurricane season).

We had worked hard and were still rebuilding our lives. We had brought up and educated our family. They were all settled, working, and heading in the right direction. The time felt right and as by chance, Thomas had asked to come and work for us for a year. He was young with a degree in Business Studies. He was also IT savvy and so good at applying it that we both ended up working together, running the business. Most importantly I trusted him to look after our people.

We had by now successfully chartered and sailed quite a few boats all around the world. My first being in 1981 when I rented a boat called *Snoopy* in Corfu, Greece. Snoop the boat had an outboard engine and I thought it would be nice for the family to potter around in. How cool was this at age thirty-one, a private villa on the beach and a yacht!

I had never sailed before but, let's face it, loads of people do it, so what could be so hard. Poking around I found the sails in a locker and strapped them on. Having decided to give it a go and with not much space, I left the engine and fuel tank on the beach and off we went.

Everyone's favourite excuse is "no one told me". It turns out that there's a big difference between inland water boats and sea-going boats. That a sailing dinghy for the sea needed a keel to make it go forwards. Poor old *Snoopy* came up short in the keel department! I'd said goodbye to Gail and left her on the beach, with the children. I told her I wouldn't be gone long, and they all waved Daddy goodbye.

When we first learned to windsurf, we found out that

leaving the beach with the wind anywhere behind you was very straightforward and so it was with Snoop Dog. As I got further out to sea and the beach was getting smaller, the waves start to bump us around. Now I'm trying to point *Snoopy* in another direction. It was like me; he didn't know how to and so didn't co-operate. The children, of course, had already lost interest in Daddy's latest idea and had gone off to swim and play on our private beach.

I spent the next six hours going sideways, down the Albanian straights and away from Corfu. The only success I had was when I got washed up on the beach off that seriously nasty little communist country, Albania. I knew this wasn't supposed to be a part of the holiday. If I landed, then I would be in all the world's newspapers for starting a major international incident. In Albania it was seriously against the law to be caught and accused of spying in a pair of Speedos. I was panicking a bit and in getting very close to the beach, I covertly hopped out into the shallow water. Pushed and pulled the Snoopy Dog so it was facing away from beach, and climbed back in.

Right, I said to myself. I had probably missed drinks time as well as lunch and it was starting to get late. There was nothing else for it other than to start again. So, I pulled on the sails, pointed the front of the boat in the direction of our lovely little Corfu villa on Avlaki beach, and hoped for the best. Blinking thing still wouldn't go in the right direction. *Snoopy* and I were getting further away from Corfu, and more towards the land where they grew spaghetti.

The sun was getting lower in the sky. Despite all that I tried; I had no control, and we were just going wherever the wind blew us. I eventually spied with my little eye, a great big and beautiful sailing yacht. It was smoothly carving its way up wind and in the middle of the straights between Albania and Corfu.

Even though it was a mile or so away I stood up and, doing aqua aerobics, waved my arms around a lot. Well done them especially the lookout who spotted my distress signal. They had changed course and were coming straight for me. They slowed and it was like they just pulled on the handbrake stopping the eighty-foot boat right next to me, in the middle of the sea, next to my little excuse for a yacht, *Snoopy*.

They turned out to be English and according to the uniforms that everyone was wearing, sponsored by Uber. The crew were immaculately dressed in black and white stripey shirts with red neckties and berets. They leaned down over the side and offered me a choice of bottled still or sparkling water along with some ropes to hold on to. They laughed when I told them I was lost and *Snoopy* was a piece of sh*t. Not that I had much choice, I asked how much it would cost and would they mind taking me back to Kassiopi to my worried wife and family. They told me that they owned Uber and not to worry as this would be a freebie. I was to put the sails away, tie the line to the bottom of the mast and to hold on tight.

Off we went for the next twenty miles at around ten knots (11mph). *Snoopy*, who had only ever dreamed of such a speed, was loving it as we planed along for the next two hours. They very kindly parked me in the Kassiopi harbour around 8pm. It was very emotional as all the crew lined the fore deck and all saluted me goodbye. I was able to walk back to Gail and the children who were by now hungry, thirsty, and therefore very relieved to see me.

Gail wasn't impressed.

As well as my first chartering experience, we had also chartered and sailed the lower parts of the Great Barrier Reef. I didn't quite understand why it was called the great Barrier reef since most of is sunk and you can't even see it. We had sailed out of Miami around the Florida Keys and out of St Vincent and around the Grenadines. Our favourite charters were in the Virgin Islands which inspired me to go further.

The Miami charter was fun. It was July and Thomas had chosen to fly home and celebrate the end of school. This left the rest of my family, Ben, Mike, Rebecca, Gail, and I, on a 45-foot sailboat. The weather was a bit moody, and we had stopped to stock up with vitals and grog at a big supermarket. Being July and way down south it was hot, humid and it poured with seasonal rain. That's an understatement. It was the same biblical rain as Noah had ordered when he was in Australia that time. It rained so hard that it swept away the doorstep drinkers, the hobos, the street sleepers as well as all the dogs and cats, which then went and blocked up the storm drains. Within thirty minutes everywhere just flooded and "everywhere" was now two feet deep in water.

By the time we reached Miami harbour and sailed away everything had started to settle down. One of the lovely things about being on a boat, is that it's always so much cooler offshore. Our second night took us south of Miami and down the Florida Keys to Key Largo. We had dropped the sails and decide to visit the yacht club for drinks and maybe dinner. We approached the harbour staying carefully in the clearly marked channel. We called them up on the VHF radio and asked for permission to enter. The reply was very polite but firm "No, sir, this is a private members' club, and you can't come in."

I was a bit taken aback, after all, I was British and had spoken in my bestest posh voice. I repeated that I was English, and that my father knew Admiral Lord Nelson very well. That we only wanted a visit, drinks and perhaps, dinner. The reply was that he was sorry, had never heard of Nelson, and that we couldn't come in. Well, I never liked rules, and never take no for an answer. I told him that I was a member of the Royal Lymington Yacht Club (not quite true, but my friend Pete was). That it's a common courtesy to always share hospitality with other sailing brothers. That for his information, Admiral Lord Nelson was famous for the battle of Trafalgar, the Nile, and for helping the Duke of Wellington beat Napoleon and then setting up my son's school.

I could tell he was getting a bit cross. He then told me he was not going to let us in and that we should vacate *his* channel immediately. Like our boat was stuck up his bottom? OK, we started to retreat. We stuck the engine gently into reverse and turned the wheel hard over to turn around. There came a nasty bump and we had hit something solid. We quickly stuck it in slow forward gear and proceeded forwards and then another nasty bump.

Gail shouted out from down below that she couldn't do her nails if we kept on bumping into things and, what was that bit of boat, floating past the window. It turned out to be the boat's rudder that it had snapped off. It transpired that the narrow-marked entrance channel had been carved out of the coral. Our going backwards and sideways had hit the coral wall, snapped the rudder clean off, and we were now, well and truly up the creak and without steerage.

Quick thinking Ben rushed forward to let the anchor drop, stopping the boat from going anywhere. After sorting ourselves out, calming down, and having a quick tot of rum, we called matey back at the private yacht club. He was not a happy bunny. We told him the problem and he sent his motorboat out to try and tow us away.

It didn't work and so the unhappy bunny who ran the door turned to the next page of his "how to run a harbour manual". Following his training and using his initiative, he decided we were a terrorist threat and called the Key Largo anti-terrorist swat team. They turned out to be busy at a July 4th barbeque and so sent Virgil the town sheriff instead. He rocked up in his fab, big patrol boat. Sirens, twin 500hp engines and a whole set of lights all flashing red, white, and blue marking the special day. Virgil was a nice guy and was really quite amused. He let it be known that the yacht club hadn't ever stumped up and contributed to the police Christmas party. For all he cared we could stay here for as long as we wanted.

It wasn't until the following day that international rescue back at Miami, sent us a new boat and took the broken one away. We had unintentionally blocked up the exit/entrance to his harbour. Some pretty big and very expensive private yachts had tried to get in and out, because of us nothing could get in or out all night. They really weren't happy. Should have let us in for drinks and dinner!

The charter company were very understanding, pocketed the $600 deposit and gave us a great big, twin hulled, power boat with a flying bridge. This was a new experience and we wanted to make the most of it. The pilot book, that is the sailing bible, said we could go very carefully into the Everglades National Park and swamps. There we would find a really cool bar. Now we had two engines and a small bottom, off we went carefully avoiding the alligators, manatees, and the mud banks which we kept getting stuck on.

Eventually we get to this outback really cool bar built on stilts sticking ten feet out of the water. It was playing loud country music and was very busy. The pride and joy boats tied up outside were gleaming, beautifully painted with huge engines that were often bigger than the boats they were on. As we came along in this great big multi hull charter boat there was a lot of very concerned rednecks. You know they're rednecks as they all have their hats on back to front and they speak really funny. They had stopped drinking and started calling out warning us not to get near their pride and joys.

We didn't want any trouble so carefully moved our boat to a nearby pontoon. Mike jumped off and took a rope line to a nearby post. We then stretched another line to the wood stilts that held up the bar. Now, Mike's not a sailor and we really needed to put some more ropes out to steady the boat. There was a lot of running about and pointing. The trouble was that the swamp river was running out towards the sea, wherever that was. This in turn meant our big boat, tied to the bar, was now pulling on its lines. We could hear the bar creaking and see that the bar was slowly being pulled over. We needed to act quickly. We were about to pull the whole bar down if we didn't just drop the lines …. real quick!

There was a lot more creaking and groaning from the stilts. Dolly Parton had stopped singing and the bar boys all put down their banjos and started a yellin' and hollerin'. As we opened the boat's throttles, it eased the load on the ropes, and the whole bar moved back on its stilts. As we closed the throttle, the current took over and again the whole bar started to pull in the other direction. It really did look to be close to collapsing.

Mike, we thought, was now doing a jig, and dancing all over the dock. He assured us, later that day, he was still trying to save the bar and more importantly, trying not to get shot at by thems good ol' boys. In the middle of all this excitement, there came that moment of clarity. Pull the bar down or abandon our crewmate. We had no choice other than to wave goodbye to Mike. In the nick of time, we threw all the boat lines into the water, let go and hoped we could find a way back to rescue our best mate.

We got lucky in somehow picking Mike up and escaping around the Florida Keys for a few more good days. On the way back we stopped again at Key Largo for a night. This time we went the other side of the island avoiding Mr Grumpy and the yacht club. Vergil, the very nice sheriff, came to visit us again. He told us that he never liked the man at the yacht club either. He did say he wasn't busy and that his next customer's water ski lesson wasn't for another hour. In exchange for a beer, he guided and so showed us where to anchor to get the best *free* views of their huge, Independence Day, fireworks display.

Eventually we returned the powered catamaran to Miami. It was on the way when we had to stop and fill up with petrol at Raoul's Gas Stop. Once I had worked out how to manoeuvre into a very tight space he came along to help. He was very polite and kept calling me captain, which I kind of liked. He filled up the first tank and told me that it was cash only and at $500. He then asked if I wanted the other tank filling!

Gail wasn't very impressed.

A Bloke Called Padi

Before buying our own boat, I thought to try out an island-hopping trip with just the two of us. In 2004 I talked my reluctant crew into flying to St Vincent and renting a boat from there. Now this was getting to be brave stuff. Just the two of us plotting a course and setting off for another island, like St Lucia, and so we did.

We dropped the hook for the first night under the St Lucian volcanoes at Soufriere. To pass through immigration you have to dinghy ashore and go and see the local plod. The day we arrived turned out to be a national holiday and the whole island was drunk and dancing in the street. It seemed to be mostly the men who were doing the Mount Gay quick step, one pace forward, two steps sideways, and one step back. This then meant that instead of walking forwards they were only ever going sideways. The really good ones made a few more steps forwards before doing the whole thing again. It was all really a bit scary with all the drunken men looking very threatening.

Once in the land of plod, we recognised the need and donated to the front middle and centre, Tips Jar. This was a still wet but now empty, Mount Gay rum bottle. That done we had cleared immigration. It took the policeman several attempts at stamping the boat's papers and our passports which in a slurred voice, he claimed kept on moving. Exhausted by the stamping and having to concentrate, he then collapsed into a chair without saying goodbye.

That night we radioed the local restaurant, and they sent a boat out to us saying it wasn't safe to be a honky, alone and wandering about that night. After dinner and later that night, we were tucked up in our double bunks as the tide turned, and the gentle wind blew from the opposite direction. The boat had swung around and started rocking left to right very badly. To begin with I just ignored it and for a while let it happen. Then the cupboard doors kept flying open and then slamming shut as stuff kept falling out. This was mad and neither of us could sleep and so we pulled up the anchor and went sailing.

As is the way, it rained, and it was cold by the time we picked up a mooring ball at Marigold Bay at around 3am. We were woken at 7.30am by someone banging on the hull. Apparently, in the dark we had tied up to a fishing pot and the boat and the fishing pot had drifted away during the night! These things happen… Gail wasn't impressed.

The following day we stopped for lunch at a place called Anse-Chastanet. This is where, fifteen years earlier, we did the Irish scuba diving course with a bloke called Padi. Back then Gail and I were the first in the family to have a go at scuba diving. After a while mucking about in the shallows, the bar had opened and Padi decided we were considered trained, certificated, and told to go and get on with it.

It was a really great experience and we wanted to share it with the children. We were certificated and considered expert padis and so I went and found a dive master. Someone who would train and take the twelve-year-old Ben and eleven-year-old Claire. This was to be their first scuba dive.

It was funny to watch them do all the swimming pool training followed by staggering down the beach with the really heavy tanks on their backs. I certainly wasn't worried about them. Let's face it, they were like a pair of fish anyway. They could both swim from an early age and every summer was spent swimming in either ours or someone else's pool. Once safely trained they were signed off and ready to go.

The dive instructor, we thought, had had a few too many dives. He was very affordable, although just a bit difficult to understand. He asked me if I had dived before, and I proudly told him about this bloke called Padi and how he had trained us. We all put on the wetsuits which in my case was a very tight fit. We polished our masks, hung our buoyancy collars around our necks and put the correct number of lead weights onto our waist straps. The instructor, who liked to be called Bubbles, asked me how much I weighed, and I replied, "one hundred and ninety pounds." I think he thought I said 190 kilos and he gave me the lead weights accordingly.

We all clambered into the boat although I was not finding it very easy with all the equipment, and the very, very heavy weights. Bubbles noticed I was struggling and looked a bit concerned. He asked me if I was sure about having done dis diving ting, before. I needed to give the children confidence and told him not to worry. He then said, "OK, papa, you go first." With my feet in the flippers and everything turned on I accidentally fell, very professionally, backwards and over the side. Of course, I had no idea that I now weighed an extra 100 kilos and not the correct 90 kilos.

Like a brick, I sank down to thirty feet before it even occurred to me that something was wrong here. It was then that I realised I had forgotten to put any air into the inflatable buoyancy collar. I reached for the emergency cord and pushed the inflate button. There was a huge rush of compressed air and I suddenly started to behave like a submarine launched nuclear rocket. Flapping my arms, I came flying, six feet, out of the water landing with an enormous splash, next to Bubbles and the kids. With the now inflated collar I looked to be twice the size as I was when I last saw them. Bubbles says, "You sure you done dis ting before?" Ben and Claire both had the giggles and I hope will always have remembered their first dive.

As a family we had spent many happy years in the St Lucian Hotel on the beautiful beach at Rodney Bay. We would be playing on the sand and from time to time a sailboat would come along and quietly just drop anchor and stay for the night. Now it was my turn to be like those other really cool adventurers.

On our way up to Rodney Bay we passed a couple of ginormous whales along the way. Up close they are so big and like sailing along with dolphins, so very exciting. On arrival we were the only boat in this lovely big bay. Returning after twenty-plus years, I wasn't sure, and it sort of didn't feel right. So not being aware of the local protocols, we moved away a bit and dropped our anchor in a quiet corner. We were in the shelter of Fort Rodders at a place called Pidgeon Point. This was one of those faraway places where, back in the day, Admiral Lord Nelson, and a few of his mates, liked to stay from time to time when they were getting it on with Napoleon.

Gail wasn't happy that we were anchored too close to the other boats. That night the wind increased, and the sea really started to get rough. All the boats were on anchor, and this made all the boats move around a lot. While this was all sort of new to us, instead of trusting myself, I was now made to feel unsure. So, to keep the peace, I had to sit up on deck all night on anchor watch. Nothing happened at least nothing that I knew about!

The following day we set off in a fresh breeze. The big main sail, which it turned out was old and rotten, split all along the leading edge making it completely useless. This charter boat was now a few years old and had been well used. There were a few other things which weren't right, that didn't work or were broken, so this wasn't helpful or going well.

Without bumping into Moby Dick, we went back to the charter company on St Vincent and gave them some grief. By way of keeping us sweet, they unwrapped, and let us have a brand new, never been used, boat. It had two steering wheels, and everything smelt like it does on a brand-new car. We felt very good and transferred our kit, bought a bag of ice, looked at the chart and off we went exploring.

Gail wasn't impressed

Living the Dream

So, there we are trundling along in the sun, listening to the Beach Boys and Jimmy Buffet playing on the deck speakers. We are up and around Mustique getting the hang of everything when we get the wake-up call. Popping out between one island and the next, it's a case of Caribbean Sea meets Atlantic Ocean. You suddenly learn that when you come out into open water, the wind increases quickly. That you must be a bit fast at getting the sails reefed down (reduced) and stopping the boat from tipping, dramatically, over on its side.

I'm braver than Gail who wasn't impressed with any of this. Sailing like this, I should have seen it coming and acted when there was plenty of time. Our problem then was that she must quickly take over and steer whilst I do what's needed. So, there I am, behaving like a young and nimble thirty-year-old climbing on top of the pitching cabin to quickly reef down the main sail.

Well, as usual we survived the terror, and the captain issued an emergency tot of rum to the whole crew. We soon got the hang of these things and carried on sailing to Bequia, Canouan, Union Island and Gap Island. These are great little places where jumbo jets don't go. They are vibrant small communities with lovely people, superb little towns, and ramshackle bars. We would either tie up on a dodgy pontoon or anchor just off the beach and dinghy ashore.

Eventually my mutinous crew and I found ourselves hanging out for a few days, in a place called Tobago Keys down near Grenada. I had some previous experience of this large area of coral reefs that are home to big turtles as well as all the other delightful snorkelling treasures that the Caribbean has to offer. My brother and I, without satellite navigation, had one time got lost in the middle of all the reefs and had tried to sink the charter boat we had rented. I didn't tell Gail!

It's an amazing little part of the Caribbean where only the lucky ones get to go. There were a few other yachties camped out and doing the same thing as us. Basically, there are lots of very small, largely uninhabited islands surrounded by miles of coral reefs. There are no buildings, no night-time lights, and clear night skies showing all the fabulous stars.

The boat boys come along each day and try to sell you the fish and lobsters they have caught. What you probably don't know is that I am professionally trained and have a certificate for cooking. I decided to try and get on the right side of my wife in this beautiful, romantic, and idyllic place, where no one we know has ever been. This boat boy comes alongside wearing an enormous lobster for a hat. He asked me for a whopping fifty dollars for the crustacean and so I tried my negotiating thing, and then paid him the fifty. Let's be honest, this far from Waitrose, fifty bucks could be considered a fair price.

The trouble was, that once onboard, it was still alive, snapping, spitting, and biting. It knew what the end game was and so wouldn't get in the bucket. It kept on trying to get out, Gail wasn't impressed. The boat is only kitted out for four people. Honestly, to get this thing from *Jurassic Park* under control, we needed a ten-player saucepan and two pairs of hands. Back in catering college Mr Burnett, our larder chef, had told us the proper way to cook a lobster was to plunge it into a saucepan of boiling water and then to cook it for fifteen minutes.

Well, the bloody thing put up one hell of a fight. We rolled all over the floor and it climbed over the bunks and swung from the compass. Every time I got it into the saucepan it got out. By now with the gas cooker at warp speed and it being thirty-two degrees outside Lob-a-Lob, and I were in a right old state. The cabin temperature was at least forty-five degrees. I was beginning to cook even if the lobster wasn't.

Eventually, being a man of action, I acted! It was him or me. I'm fifty bucks down and bugger the animal rights people. I grabbed the wire cutters and started to fight back snipping off more and more of its tentacles and claws. Eventually I managed to get the lid on the cooking pot and even then, it still tried to get out. It seemed like a horrible and cruel way to treat any animal and I will never do that again. Lob-a Lob had the last laugh though. He didn't even taste nice and I'm sure from that point forwards, he placed a curse on the boat and us.

Hungry and grumpy, we set off the next day, following in the wake of a great big American naval boat that was passing through. Gail, who was driving had noticed we were steering erratically. As captain I took over and, as she so often is, she was right. Gradually the steering wheel was making more and more dramatic movements, and the boat wasn't responding. We turned on the engine and dropped the sails. The steering still wasn't responding, and we were definitely not in control. You can steer a little bit by using the sails but only if the wind is in the right direction, which it wasn't. We dropped the anchor, always a good idea to bring things to a halt whilst we work out what to do.

Down and down went the big anchor knocking out several turtles and killing goodness knows how many basking fish. It got to 100ft, and it made no difference, the actual depth being 300ft. The crew were frightened, and so common sense was to put on the lifejackets, making sure the dinghy was attached and ready to go. We grabbed all the essentials like passports, wallets, phones and, of course, the Mount Gay, in case we had to abandon ship.

I popped a few boards looking for the problem. The rudder on the brand-new boat had come apart from the steering gear and the emergency rudder had no effect. We were being pushed by the wind and tide onto the outer reef of Union Island. I couldn't see a way in which we could get out of this, and the trailing anchor was still looking for something to grab onto. We used the VHF radio repeatedly to radio for help, but no one was responding.

We were drifting towards Union Island and the reef that surrounded the harbour entrance. Our charter company had an agent at the boathouse there and as we got nearer, we eventually got a phone signal. We called the number given but this was only 11am on island time. That meant they were still in bed and of course they didn't pick up.

Things were getting a bit desperate, and I really didn't have any options. The wind and tide were still pushing us towards the reef which was now less than half a mile away. Since no one else wanted to talk to us I desperately phoned the charter base back at St Vincent, sixty miles away. The nice lady who picked up was, I think, cleaning the bar. When I told her we were going to die, she panicked and screamed running to get someone else.

The conversation was brief. I told them we were half a mile northeast of Union Island without any form of steering or control. That any time soon their brand-new boat was going to be wrecked upon the reef. No one was responding to our SOS and that in ten minutes we were going to get into the dinghy and save ourselves. They said not to panic and that we should take extra care. The coral reef was listed as endangered and protected by order of David Attenborough. On no account then were we to damage it! They said to make a cup of tea and that they would try and get someone out to us as quickly as possible.

After nine minutes, as we were getting ready to abandon ship, two blokes in their pyjamas came tanking out of the harbour. They were clutching the paperwork for all and any salvage rights and their two 500hp engines were alight and on full after burners.

At the very last minute we were saved from the curse of Lob-a-Lob. We got towed back into the harbour and put ashore while they went about fixing the boat. It had been a long and stressful morning and, more importantly, we had missed drinks time. Understandably Gail lashed out and really went for the two boys as well as me.

I put it all down to be another great adventure which had all turned out quite well in the end. Gail, however, refused to get back on the boat leaving me with another new problem. To be fair, the charter company didn't have a leg to stand on. They refunded all our money and the deposit. This then left us with all our bags, marooned on a Caribbean island.

The return flight back to the UK was from St Lucia. We weren't talking at this point. I decided, if we were going to divorce, then needing somewhere to live, I had better go to the British Virgin Islands and buy a boat. To get out of Union Island we needed to take a small local twin-engine island-hopping aeroplane. They are like buses servicing all the small islands.

The young pilot, in Bermuda shorts and an airline T-shirt, climbed in and introduced himself as Buzz. Having welcomed us to the ride of a lifetime, he cranked up the two engines and turned his hat around backwards so, he claimed, he could see better.

Lighting up the throttles he shouted for us all to hang on and went for it. The amazing little aeroplane went 150 yards and then, like Apollo 13, headed straight for the moon. We were pushed right back in our seats staring at the tree lined volcano now filling up the windscreen in front of us. Buzz Lightyear, however, called out above the noise of the screaming engine, not to worry, "I do this every day." No sooner had we rocketed up the vertical face of the first mountain, we then had to dive down super hard into the next valley. Hidden behind the first volcano was another, even higher one, that we hadn't seen from the ground. The little plane was vibrating like mad and the engines revving like a flat out Lambretta motor scooter. Once the critical speed reached a special number on the clocks, Buzz pulled the 'joystick' back and with a whoop, over we went.

I imagine Gail, who still wasn't speaking to me, was probably not very impressed and wondering when all this adventuring and terror would finally come to an end. On the other hand, I thought, this was so much better than going to Legoland with the grandchildren.

Eventually, after having the sails fall apart in St Lucia, run aground in Bequia, been attacked by jellyfish in Canouan, rescued from sinking on the reef at Union Island, attacked by a giant lobster in Tobago Kays, we arrived on Tortola in the British Virgin Islands.

We were going through one of those phases of married life where the 'bag on' lasts for several days. Given all the near-death experiences that we had 'survived' in the previous two weeks I should have realised, Gail doesn't want to go sailing. Well, I wasn't in the mood and had already been in touch with the yacht brokers on the island. They rebuilt and restored five-year-old charter boats that had reached the end of rental life expectancy.

With two US dollars to the pound this was a great time to buy. Over several days I went and visited different boats being restored. Finally, I had the pick of four used and rebuilt boats. It felt important to just sit on each of them and get to know the boats. That way you got a feeling for the detail, comfort and all the little pieces before choosing which one I would like. I settled for a fully equipped 42ft sailboat named *Life of Reilly*. It had three double cabins, two bathrooms, a saloon with dining table and all. There was a proper forward-facing chart table with lots of knobs and switches to play with. As an ex-charter boat, it was now sold fully equipped and ready to go having everything it needed. Sheets, pillows, pots and pans, safety equipment, the lot, but sadly not the Mount Gay Rum.

After a few days on a sun lounger Gail and I decided, once again, that we weren't going to divorce. We flew home on Virgin Atlantic whilst the boatyard carried on with the final details. We went to our hacienda in Spain and enjoyed the summer. As with anything new and different, the excitement mounted. We soon had to go and collect the newly refurbished boat and get on with our next adventure. Once again Gail was very good, plucked up courage and threw herself into my next adventure.

They say rich people have a lot of their money 'offshore'. The Virgin Islands are a collection of little islands, with very few people and very good weather. It's clearly a good place to bury some of your dirty money. Getting there is not very easy unless you are loaded. The rich geezers phone up and order their private yachts to the nearest and most convenient international airport.

They hop aboard, tell the captain where to go and party on. In the mornings after breakfast, anchored off their secret island hideaways, they get off and go dig up some more of their wonga.

Like us, if you're not that well off then you fly BA to Antiqua. You then find the Liat desk then try and pretend your luggage only weighs 15kg before boarding a number seven small prop plane. It's a bit like a bus and stops all the way around the islands as people jump on and fall off. Finally, we get to the boatyard on Virgin Gorda and spend our first night onboard our own private yacht.

In the five years that followed we spent a total of eighteen months sailing around the islands. Hoping she would be impressed; I had newly named our boat *Gail Force* after my favourite wife. Gail was getting really good at jumping from the boat to the pontoon. When getting into a marina, this was important, tying on the ropes and quickly securing the boat and stopping it from going somewhere else. I had bought her a really nice pair of sparkly deck shoes in an effort to get her to protect her feet.

She didn't listen to me and so this all came to a head when in Spanish Town she jumped… straight onto the metal deck, in a boatyard. It was the Caribbean, the middle of the day, very hot and so was the deck. Gail was always such a good dancer! and somehow survived burnt feet. For a long time after, she wore the nice shoes I had bought her.

She was also dead good at leaning out from the front of the boat and picking up mooring balls with the boat hook. They are tied to the seabed and don't move. They have a little trailing line with a hooped end. It was Gails job the catch a hold of the hoop, pull it onboard and hook it over the anchor winch. It's what you called the carrot and stick approach. Hooking us on was a precursor to drinks and a swim, so hooking on usually went very well and was done quickly!

In all we sailed to all the Virgin Islands. To Antigua, St Kitts, Nevis, Saba, St Marten, and St Croix. The American boarder police are such a pain, so we sneaked into and out of the tiny American Islands of St Johns and St Thomas. This is where we met up with Mike and Marylin our boating friends. They came for the day sober and left very drunk, on a cruise boat called the *Costa Fortuna*. After a day drinking Rum Punches in this really good bar. We waved them goodbye as we struggled to find our dinghy and they staggered up the gang plank, back to their

state room. It wasn't so easy for us. I took a long while to get Gail up off the pontoon floor, into the dinghy and back onboard our "little cruise" boat *Gail Force*.

We eventually made it back to one of our favourite anchorages, Willy Wonka Bay on the island of Virgin Gorda. It was renamed when we woke up there one day to a phone call from Roman telling us, proudly, that Rebecca had popped out our first grandchild, a little boy called William. A big moment for us which meant that we had to park the boat up and rush back to Switzerland in record time.

It was here that on another occasion while sailing around the islands, we were woken up one morning at seven thirty with someone banging on the hull. The wind was blowing hard, and the sky was a horrible storm-coming grey. In the wind the boats had dragged on their anchors and were getting tangled up. Sometimes on a boat, you have to react quickly to a situation. I needed to start the engine and take control of the boat which was now pitching around all over the place.

It was a difficult situation and Gail bravely and quickly responded. She ran up the front to pull the anchor up on its electric winch. The thunder and lightning by now had kicked in and the storm was crashing and banging right above us. It was super scary and afterwards we realised just how dangerous it all was for Gail. Up front in her Pyjamas, surrounded by all the metal rigging running to the top of the mast. The wire guard rails and the 100 feet of anchor chain!

There were so many more things that happened to us during our time. On one occasion we had dived of the back of the boat while we were tied onto a mooring ball. We were recharging the batteries and had the engine running. In doing so I knocked the engine into gear which then resulted in our boat happily motoring along, around and around the mooring ball. We were of course still swimming around and I'm not a great swimmer. I'm saying to Gail your faster you go after the boat which believe me was pretty near on impossible. We got lucky as a neighbouring boat had seen us as a pair of plonkers and came whizzing over in a dinghy to rescue the boat and then us!

For a brief moment in time, we were even famous and

featured in an article called 'Living the Dream' for *Practical Boat Owner*.

We also took part in the Mount Gay sailing Regatta where we came home in last place. We would have been disqualified anyway for drinking and driving as well as playing such terrible music, very loudly.

Our favourite Sunday brunch venue was at the lovely Bitter End resort at the top end of one of the islands. On the beach, it kicked off at 11.00am and finished when all the champagne, lobster and prime rib had run out.

People ask me if I miss the boat and at times I do. It's like so many of the things that I have seen and done. A lovely memory to think back on.

What I do know is that it's not bad for a toilet roll salesman.

King Richard

Whilst hanging around the beach, we had met this good fun guy Richard and his newly acquired boat, Touché. Before taking on paying guests, he needed some help in giving his new investment a shakedown journey. At the same time, he intended to collect some of his possessions from a boatyard in Antigua. He was a bit unsure of himself and so I offered to go with him as unpaid crew. As is the way with a mini adventure I was very excited about getting away. It was to be a straightforward round trip from Trellis Bay, on the British Virgin Islands, to Jolly Harbour on the western side of Antigua.

I had left my wife Gail on the boat dock of the aptly named Bitter End Hotel. This was our favourite property on the north of an island named Virgin Gorda. The leaving was indeed 'bitter'. We had argued a couple of days before and things had not been going well. Now for the first time, Gail had to take control of our rather tatty, heavily patched but newly glued together inflatable dinghy. On leaving, like a plonker I'd left the oars somewhere else and so, getting anywhere was all down to luck and our old and tatty Daihatsu outboard engine.

It had been playing up a bit and giving trouble after the engine had tried to escape on a trip between one of the other islands. We were still learning how everything worked and didn't appreciate that all things on a boat are stubborn and have a mind of their own. We were sailing along and towing the dinghy behind. The little devil managed to loosen its retaining bolts and make a run for it. Without saying anything to us, it threw itself over the back of the rocking and rolling dinghy. Fortunately, I am not completely 'doo-lally' and had the good sense to put on an engine safety strap for situations such as this. This stopped the engine from visiting Davy Jones's locker which, as you know, is located somewhere down on the seabed.

Gail, however, always spots the problem. We stop the boat and drag the drowned engine back onto the boat. Clearly, any sort of drowning is serious, so we rushed it to an old Afro-Caribbean doctor. Whilst not speaking Japanese, he at least understood what to do and what medication to give the Far Eastern runaway. Finally, an hour and a half and fifty dollars later we were told the good news. The Daihatsu, which had survived Pearl Harbour, the battle of Midway, and many other encounters, would pull through.

Daihatsu, this apparently is his name, was in recovery and beginning to regain most of his normal functions. Over the summer of 2008 and during a period of convalescence, Daihatsu received more medication and one-to-one counselling from a nice man called 'Trinidad'. Clearly, they had bonded. On a steady diet of US dollars, Daihatsu gradually calmed down, becoming a little less homesick than he was. Probably in looking around, he had seen a lot of his fellow countrymen working out here in the islands. This of course helped him through the period of readjustment and ultimate recovery.

Gail was going to stay aboard our boat, safely fixed to a mooring ball, near to the hotel. She was dropping me off at the boat dock to catch the ferry to Trellis Bay on Tortola Island. The idea was that I would call her each day to make sure everything was all right. As we got close, Gail had a problem with the dinghy. At the moment of docking our dinghy decided to hump a topless Italian dinghy called *Lu-Lu*.

While all this was going on, I had jumped out onto the dock. There was no time as the ferry boat was now starting to pull out. It was already very emotional. In a moment of panic Gail had no choice but to throw the all-important mobile phone cable to me. Throw high I shouted, and Gail threw low. The cable snaked away over the pontoon on its way to see the pretty little fishes, four feet down on the sandy seabed.

The captain of the ferry looked at us in a way that professional seamen do. He said something like "youse a messing or comin'?" as he dropped the boat lines and opened the throttles. As they say, time and tide wait for no one, and I had to go. Without the cable the only way we could keep in touch was now reduced to the time left on one good battery cycle. Gail was now left, all alone, on a boat, somewhere in the Caribbean.

She was left crying, and I had no proper way to keep in touch with her. I sat for the whole journey on the back of the noisy ferryboat as it roared along kicking up great plumes of spray. There was nothing more to be said or done and really, we needed the time apart. It just wasn't the right way to leave.

Captain Richard (Dick to his friends) was waiting for me at the public dock on Trellis Bay. With the wind blowing strongly, we swapped dinghy lines for lifejackets and harnesses and set off. *Touché* is a big chunky 52-foot American built sloop (one main mast, two front sails and a big mainsail). It looked a bit like what you had in the bath when you were little. Ready to go we hauled up the anchor which wasn't as easy as it should have been. Captain Dick as ever got covered in poo and degraded further his remaining, single pair of serviceable shorts. Unknowingly, he then spent the next twenty-four hours going around with his testicles hanging out.

We were setting off on a fine and sunny Monday morning. It's a straight-line distance of 180 miles to Antigua. As our luck would have it, the wind that day was right on the nose. A southeasterly trade wind, blowing happily at 15-20 knots. Since you can't sail a sailboat directly into the wind, our plotted course then had to be quite a bit longer. You can't always sail in straight lines on a sailboat. Sometimes you must sail at angles to the wind. This is what is called 'tacking'. We began at forty-five degrees away from the direction we needed to travel in. It adds sea miles and time to the journey, but such is the way when you are sailing. Two steps forwards and one step back. That evening we were finally surrounded by sea and no sight of land. The sun did its bit and put on a show by gracefully slipping down into the clouds below the western horizon.

In my opinion, when you are quietly out at sea, alone and with nothing else in sight, a beautiful sunset, the sound of the boat and the sea is really powerful. The magnitude size and scale of everything is very humbling. We are so small, and the world is so big. For me every sunset is a quiet moment of reflection.

The night slowly settled in, as it does. The boat was pounding along safely, even if in the wrong direction, in a strong twenty knots of wind. As the darkness enveloped us the phosphorous spewed out into the dark sea with every rise and fall of the boat. If you've not seen this phenomenon, it's caused by a type of plankton. When agitated the plankton reacts in the water like fireworks. They are alight, alive, and streaming a flashing bright trail beside and behind the boat as it ploughed along at six knots. As a precaution we had reefed down and reduced the sails for night-time sailing. Richard, with his balls still hanging out, prepared and cooked an excellent meal from scratch. He's a bit fond of his extra special little add-ins which, as best as I can make out, would not really bother Jamie Oliver.

By 10pm we decide to go into night watch routine. Two hours on, then two hours in your bunk asleep. My first watch was midnight through 2am. I had given up trying to sleep in the front double cabin. It's hard to be comfortable let alone sleep when you're being rolled around on what's supposed to be a double bed. I imagine it is like being in a washing machine. As we got further away from land, the seas were getting a little rough. We were beating headfirst into the wind and the boat was rising and falling as it cut through the waves. Whilst it's quite normal, there was a lot of sea spray, flying fish and stuff coming over the front of the boat and in through the leaking front hatch over my bed.

It's standard practice at night so we sensibly agreed to put on lifejackets and harnesses. The conditions, whilst not frightening, were windy. The boat was well heeled over to the point that caution and care was sensible. We settled in to watch the stars and keep a lookout for other boats of which we only saw one. Staying awake was not a problem on the first night and the moon poked its head up above the horizon around 2am. It's amazing how even a little moon really does light up the darkness and the seas around you.

The spooky bit is, with the moon's light, you get to see the waves. Worst of all are the odd breaking waves which sometimes come from a slightly different direction, straight at the side of the boat. Although huddled up and safe, you think you're going to get wet. You instinctively duck down and most of the time the boat, of course, just rises up over the wave without drama. Gradually you settle into the rhythm and get used to it. Then 'bosh', before you know it, you're wet! Fortunately, it's not serious although it just makes you jump which in turn helps to keep you wet, alert and awake.

It wasn't until daylight later that morning that we noticed the canoe was missing. It was there when I turned in! Richard had bought and fitted some serious steel brackets to hold it to the outside of the boat. In the dark we had taken a hit from a few of the bigger waves. On a boat there is always some banging and crashing going on when you are sailing so close to a strong wind. We guessed that like my outboard engine the canoe had decided to take its chances and bugger off back to the Virgin Islands.

As the day wore on *Touché*, now minus the canoe, was starting to show her age. By midday we had to stop the boat in the middle of the ocean to sort out the davits on the back of the boat. They were holding onto the rubber dinghy, our life raft, which had taken a bit of a bashing on the back of the boat. At some time in the past the brackets had been welded back together. However, like an ageing old lady, they had begun to sag and finally now, to start coming apart. To stop the dinghy dragging in the water we decided to take the dinghy into tow. Somehow, I got the first of what seemed like many short straws. I now found myself in the middle of the ocean, precariously balancing in the dinghy, partly hanging from the davits and with no bung to stop the water coming in the stern of what was now a sinking dinghy.

Whilst lighting up another cigarette, Captain Richard was managing the situation from the safety of the boat. He pointed out that under the boat was one mile of deep water complete with some not very friendly big fish. A lot of water was now coming into the sinking dinghy. It became a rush job to get the pulleys and tangled lines free before me and the dinghy also went down to Davy Jones's locker. Another problem, of course, was that the rubbing metalwork had now caused a puncture to our life raft. The dinghy was all lopsided and more liable to being swamped. This then was the second of Richard's little jokes. We, of course, survived and finally got the job done. I was pleased to climb back onto the safety of *Touché*, as we resumed our journey.

By afternoon the wind had started to kick up some more and so we started the process of putting in another reef in the main sail. This helps to keep the boat upright and makes it easier for Jack (the automatic pilot) to keep control. On *Touché*, to do this you have to again take your life in your hands. Go up on pitching and rolling deck to the foot of the mast. Here you find countless bundles of rope that control all the sails, as well as three winches. This time it's Richard's turn. After pulling, pushing, rocking, and rolling there is finally a really big bang. It was like a gun shot. For a moment we weren't sure what had gone wrong. Eventually we notice the first reefing line to the main sail had in fact broken.

With the boat stationary (heaved to), the wind was getting stronger. The sea was rolling us around as we worked out that, at the mast, we in fact have a bigger problem. The reefing lines, that when pulled in make the sail smaller, are all in a muddle and have been put on wrongly. So, the wind is by now really quite strong and instead of having a smaller more controllable sail it's either all the sail or nothing. It's too dangerous and so there's nothing that we can do, pitching around, to restring the boat. We have to keep the boat moving forwards and so we settle for all the main sail and just the smaller of the two front sails.

Nothing is ever easy on a boat. We were bouncing along and beginning to wonder what else could possibly go wrong. Bob the sailmaker is a bit like a little Lofthouse elf. He clearly hadn't heard of Specsavers. When the sail was sent for cleaning one of his little helpers had missed a couple of small holes along the back of the sail. Well needless to say, the little holes we had started our adventure with, had by now become one very big hole rendering the front sail completely useless.

All things considered Captain Dick had another thinking cigarette before making a snap decision which was to start the engine and motor. Quite sensible given the useless front sail and an oversized main sail with a hole in it. You can't make this stuff up. Would you believe it, the engine started, coughed, spluttered, and then died. I know it was daytime but by now, I was wearing my lifejacket, harness and started fearing the worst. Richard on the other hand, seemed to have a lot of faith in Dave, the bloke who sold him this boat. Honestly, I wasn't so sure.

The engine steadfastly refused to run properly. Richard has fifty gallons of spare fuel under the floorboards. Our first assessment was that we had run out of diesel. Our second guess was that there was water in the fuel. Apparently, water is heavier than diesel and so water sinks to the bottom of the fuel tank. We thought chucking ten gallons of the good stuff in would do no harm and might even help out, and so we did.

The engine ran for a bit and after a few minutes gave up again. St Maarten, half Dutch, and half French was ten miles away to windward. We had to get out of the weather and the rough sea, drop anchor somewhere whilst we sorted things out. After three careful hours we gently sailed into the big cruise boat harbour. We were so hoping that this would be Dutchland where nice people will always try to help you. The worst case of course was that we were in Frogland where they would probably just lock us up and we would never be seen again.

Once in the shelter of the bay we were able to calm down, relax a little and to try things again. We cranked up the engine. Thank goodness and for some strange reason it liked the new and improved fuel cocktail. Quickly and before it stopped again, we motored into the nearest marina and tied up on the fuel dock. Rasta Master came rushing out onto the pontoon waving his arms, dancing, and shouting. He must have been Dutch since we couldn't understand a word of what he was saying. Captain Richard wasn't daft and turned off the engine. Slipping him twenty US dollars, he explained that everything possible had broken. That we couldn't and shouldn't move until we had made the repairs. Again, we had no idea what he said but he just up and 'jived' his way back to wherever he kept his stash. We got on with the process of repairing, changing, and fixing *Touché* for the last leg of our journey to Antigua.

We had lost the canoe somewhere in the dark. The all-important life raft had a puncture and was half deflated. The bent brackets we removed for a later fix. The front sail was rotten and torn beyond repair. The reefing lines we were able to remove and replace properly. Another man, Rasta Diesel, came and emptied our contaminated fuel tank. We replaced the filters, so the engine was now back in business. We patched up the dinghy with some band aid for boats and got some air back into it. The bedding was hung out to dry. We were ready to go, and all was back together.

By sunset we were off on our way again. In poking around we had found a little storm sail buried in a locker. This was now rigged up as the working front sail. We could manage with one less reefing line and a full tank of new diesel. The crippled dinghy needed a proper blow job which would have to wait until we arrived in Antigua. It was, however, now bouncing along behind us having a good laugh at our slow progress.

The wind in the shelter of the harbour was quite calm. Now as we pushed out it was again getting stronger and still not from the right direction. That night we fairly blew past St Kitts and St Barts. To get an island named after you, you had to be a gung-ho missionary a very long time ago. Basically, you turned up, said hello, and then got eaten by the locals. For that they called you a saint and usually named the island after you.

Richard came up with another dinner, cooked while sailing along at forty-five degrees. (That's roughly the angle that the boat heels over at and not the oven temperature.) Since we were able to see the loom of the lights from Antigua on the horizon, we cracked on choosing not to sleep.

We were using the admiralty sailing chart for the area. Like proper salty sea dogs, with the help of the dividers and a packet of Fisherman's Friends, we estimated our arrival to be at 9am the next morning. Then, as things do when on a long voyage, the wind shifted to the north and dropped, as did our boat speed. We now had to tack away from Antigua to get the sailing angle and the wind into Jolly Harbour right. This then meant revising our arrival time to first 2pm then 6pm and then finally 2am. What a slog, eventually we were able to start the engine, turn into the wind dropping the sails and anchor at 4am in ten feet of water. After being blown and thrown around for three days it was now, in an instant, so lovely and quiet as well as calm.

It was the middle of the night, and we were very tired. Not wanting to insult Antigua we decided it would be rude not to have a drink. We toasted the island, each other, and the rotten and leaking *Touché*. We easily dropped into our beds for what then remained of the night. By the time we had arrived we had travelled 350 miles from the island of the Virgins. The straight line on the chart had it as one hundred and eighty-five miles. In all that way we only saw three pilot whales. No dolphins, and nothing else exciting. I think this is unusual as well as very disappointing.

Strange Antiguan Customs

The following day was as if the last three days had never happened. Funny, but Captain Richard has this charter company all set up. It's named 'On Deck BVIs'. This was the shake down trip and now Richard thinks he can take paying clients out and around the Caribbean on this rather sad, tired, and leaking old boat! The only 'on deck' bit that I can see was because everything must come up on deck to dry out.

Later in that day we tied up at the Jolly Harbour customs dock and cleared in. They are a funny old lot. Give 'em a badge and a job for life, a uniform and suddenly they become very important and lose their sense of humour. After the journey we just had, we needed a laugh as wobbled up the steps. There's the man just sitting in one little room all chilled out with the radio playing. He's the big cheese customs officer. He gives you a form to fill in but no pen.

You are then sent next door to see an immigration lady with a big black and white television showing *I Love Lucy*. It's not that Antigua's backward, it just they can't afford TV programmes that were made after the 1960s. Whilst I found the programme funny, you have to be honest and accept that it was really rather bad. Anyways, she stamps the form and your passport and then sends you back to the first man with the radio.

He takes your form again, checks the stamp and then sends you to the cashier at the end of the block. She's not as important as lady number one and has a smaller TV. Protecting her turf, she won't share her TV privilege with us or let us see what's on? Richard, always one step behind, hasn't got any Eastern Caribbean dollars, so I have to pay up. We and the all-important, now much travelled form, go back to see the first man again. You can get the ladies to smile but not 'this little puffed-up big man' who finally agrees to let us and the boat into the promised land of Antigua.

After three days pumping the fuel out, filter and sail changes it became time to leave. We had patched, repaired, and blew up the dinghy/lifeboat tying it firmly and securely across the back of the boat. If we were to sink or to have to abandon ship then the dinghy might not now be a quick, ready to go option!

Captain Richard had now decided, at a moment's notice, to sail us further down south on the island to Plymouth Harbour. At Jolly Harbour we were moored 200 metres from customs and the refuelling dock. Instead of doing the smart thing, refuelling, and taking on much needed fresh water and then clearing out. We had to leave it to the last minute and go, in a hurry, somewhere else further down the island, to Plymouth harbour! I really think this had more to with the fact that we hadn't paid our three days of mooring fees. A covert, quick departure was more within Captain Richard's budget which of course had lately taken a bit of a bashing. So, off we go again.

Having arrived, the ever-forward-thinking captain, Richard now decided to take a look at the pilot book to find the location of Customs and Immigration. Guess what, it wasn't in Plymouth Harbour where we had dropped anchor. It was around the corner in Nelson's Dockyard, the next bay along. To make matters worse, once we did get there, the customs shed had nowhere to tie the boat up to. You either swam or dinghied ashore to see the important big little people with TVs, badges, uniforms, and radios. Since our dinghy was firmly tied up to the back of the boat like an oven-ready turkey, we were stuffed.

Captain Dick lit up a fag. In an inspirational cloud of nicotine-loaded smoke, he decided we should quickly return to Jolly Harbour, where we had just escaped from. Looking at the watch, this then meant a bit of a race. Although there was a customs dock there we should be concerned. There would probably be an arrest warrant out for stealing a government pen, non-payment of harbour dues and spying on a government owned TV.

We had two hours and 12 miles to cover before they closed at 4pm. This was brilliantly achieved, even though we of course encountered another drama on route. We had a 'man overboard' fender that had not been tied on properly and now needed rescuing. We needed the MOB practice. Even though we were on the edge timewise, Richard said it would cost twenty dollars to get a new one and therefore had to be done…

As it said in the book, before arriving, we were told to raise the customs people at Antigua, on the VHF radio. Despite our best efforts, I guess the noise from all the radios and TVs drowned it out, so they did not respond. We fronted up at 3.50pm with ten minutes to go. Radio man (customs) had gone home early. Seriously, TV woman (immigration) was doing a perm to some stranger's hair on the front porch. The cashier's legs could be seen sticking out from under her desk where she was now sleeping off her Mount Gay lunch. We were then told, that it was Saturday and so people tended to go home early!

I really went off on one. As well as other things I told them repeatedly, using all my best English swear words, what a waste of time they all were. How they let themselves, Antigua, and most importantly Her Imperial Majesty the Queen down. I'm not sure if I should go back again anytime soon, to this outpost of the British Empire. It took me a half hour walking around the building site to calm down. Because of Captain Dick, instead of being on our way back to the island of Virgins 180 miles up north, we now had to spend another night in Antigua.

I was determined to make the really good Sunday brunch at the Bitter End Hotel. As my phone battery finally ran out, I had told Gail I was hoping to be back in time for some decent food and loads of André champagne which flows freely all through brunch. It's not really champagne. It comes in a look-alike bottle with a foil top and a plastic cork. It's Californian which you buy in the supermarket for $5 and at the hotel for thirty-five dollars. It comes freely with the brunch and is very good for cleaning up your old paint brushes.

Although I had signed on as crew, I think by this time I really had had enough. I had worked really hard at fixing and keeping everything going. I had managed the rather slow, unthinking Captain Richard with his balls hanging out. We had the boat ready to leave on Saturday and now, because he didn't want to pay the harbour fees, we can't leave.

Finally, on Sunday morning, we went and paid the now breakfast-eating, radio-playing customs official and his hareem. At the fuel dock, Captain Richard had been arrested for not paying his three days' docking fees. Once he had explained how it had slipped his mind and that with good conscience he had returned to pay. The big Black geezer who owned the dockyard unpadlocked the boat and said he would look forward to the next time. We refuelled and did the freshwater thing and were finally on our way.

Unlike on the way down, for the return journey we were on the opposite end of the same wind that had made us so slow on the way down. It was blowing favourably from the right direction, southeast up the chuff (back of the boat). We knew we were in for a good journey and had changed the little storm sail for the really big, newly repaired genoa that goes on the very front. This would pull us along giving us easy and excellent speed. The purpose of this trip was so Richard could try out his new boat and to collect his personal possessions. In amongst all that clobber was his fishing gear that had come across the Atlantic on another sailboat.

Fishermen are, of course, another strange old lot. Despite everything we had been through in the week that we had been away, just as soon as we were in clear water then out it all comes. We were now Captain Birdseye, sporting expensive fishing rods all sticking out either side of *Touché*. Five miles out and Richard took the 'lure' out of its cage. It was a really angry looking, make-believe squid with great big eyes. He tied it onto the line then threw it into the sea. Bang, it immediately bit a fish and didn't let go. Once landed and ceremoniously bashed on the head with the ice hammer, it showed itself to be a Spanish mackerel a long way from home. Fortunately, I speak a little Spanish having a property on the Costa del Sol. This was, of course, most helpful in finding out the fishes name (pescado) and what brand of fish this was before it expired.

Since Octopussy, the beady eyed lure, was still full of fight, he got thrown in again for more combat. This time he bit into a bloody great tuna (well, I thought it was big). This one did not need a translator being of the common local type. Once bashed, it was into the bucket and before you could say ketchup, Octopussy was back over the side for more.

I presume after such a long day he was slowing down and really had to struggle to make the next catch. This was a two-foot-long yellowfin tuna. I was getting the idea about how this sport, 'Fish and Bash', worked and into the bucket he went. The bucket was by now very crowded. Richard put the catch into the fridge in a carrier bag with our remaining ice cubes. This caused me a little concern since I was hoping to have it with my rum ration, later that day.

That night the wind was blowing up to thirty-five knots and

still 'up the chuff'. This is gale force eight stuff and can be quite tricky. However, the boat was making between seven and eight knots with the waves coming from behind giving us a power boost. Since it was now dark, we had rigged for caution and had reefed the sails down appropriately. By morning, without any dramas, we could see Richard Branson's house on Virgin Gorda and the end of our journey. Twenty-four hours start to finish felt like we had set a record for the fastest sailboat trip from Antigua to the Virgin Islands.

There had been no sight of the canoe either then or since. As we sailed upwind along the eastern side of the island of Virgin Gorda, *Touché* had the last laugh. We were probably tired and careless. As we turned out of the wind the front sail ropes flapped around and destroyed the radar reflector hanging in the shrouds at the side of the boat. Thinking that's another fifty dollars gone and close to tears, Richard dropped me at our boat, *Gail Force*, in The Bitter End Sound and went off to anchor somewhere. It being Monday meant that we had missed our Sunday Brunch, but we were once again talking and back on the same page. We settled down for a delicious, self-caught tuna with ginger and garlic, dinner and a very good night's sleep.

Some weeks later we caught up with poor old Richard wearing a new pair of shorts. His problems continued. Whilst sailing his second lot of paying customers, the prop shaft and propellor completely fell out of his boat and disappeared to the bottom of the Caribbean Sea. In part he was very lucky. It was only a wooden bung, quickly hammered into the leaking prop shaft hole, that prevented the whole boat from sinking.

Good old Richard has suggested we should sail to Venezuela next!

Golf – That Sinking Feeling

It was around this time in our 'grown up lives' that we started to play golf. Back in the day and for work, I would have reason to go to the cash and carry. This was to buy products we couldn't really buy elsewhere. I got to buying other stuff that I fancied even though it had nothing to do with work. It was always worse when Gail came along since we ended up with all sorts of things we never even knew existed. Typical us, we just couldn't resist a bargain such as buying two sets of Tony the Tiger golf clubs. It must have been on one of their monthly special BOGOF deals (Buy-One-Get-One-Free) and sponsored by the great Tiger himself.

I reasoned that golf can't be that hard, as loads of people we know do it. Now we had the golf clubs, we had better book some lessons and go shopping. My sleeping partner said we needed to buy exotic-coloured golf-only costumes, shoes, waterproofs, golf trolleys, gloves, hats and so on.

For our first paid lesson, Rhino, our new golf pro instructor, showed us how to get into all the packaging and helped peel off all the sticky stuff on the new clubs. We found out that Rhino was only his stage name and that before golf, he was a hairdresser called Jason. With his help it wasn't long before we could stand properly, hold onto the club without letting it go, and to hit the balls off the nylon mats on the practice range.

It was only a few weeks later that we started going to big, pay and play golf courses. We looked amazing in plus four trousers, V-neck stripey tank tops and oversized, soft golfing caps. I now realise that the bloke in the golf pro shop had seen us coming in and used the moment to close his shop temporarily. He said this was so he could 'look after us properly', which he did. I'm sure he was a big fan of Frank Spencer and some of the items he sold us were still priced in pounds, shillings, and pence!

By now we were reading books about Tiger Woods and how he plays every shot. We also started using the new vocabulary we had picked up. Fade, draw, mulligans, lob, loft, wedge and most importantly four. Now, shouting "FOUR" was the most widely used golfing word in the book. When you whack the ball and it goes completely in the wrong direction, you shout "FOUR", as loudly as you can. All the other players on the course, who hear the call, jump into the nearest bush, bunker, or rabbit hole to avoid getting clobbered.

Fully kitted out we were smacking golf balls all over Surrey and loving every minute of it. I had moved on to a new electric golf buggy and a super pro, Tiger Woods, golf bag to put all my clobber in. The bloke in the pro shop told me how well we were doing and how this new equipment would improve my game.

Now we felt ready to become part of this elite community and so I applied to join Windlesham golf club. We were invited to go along for an interview and so we went along dressed up to impress the club captain. Finding a parking space wasn't so easy because of all the builders, plumbers, and roofing company vans. It wasn't because they were working there, it turns out they were all the members out playing the game. They asked us to fill in a form and did we have a bank account. When I told them yes, they replied, "Very well, that's good," and, "please write us a cheque." We were now respectable members.

They were a bit tougher at the old well-established club, East Berks. I had to be proposed and vetted by the then captain. I spent the night before my interview reading up on top spin, golf etiquette and how to add up a Stapleford score card. Entering the club's office, I was quickly escorted to meet El Capitano who was sitting, wearing a green jacket, plus fours and shiny brown shoes with holes in to let the smell out.

I stood to attention, called him 'sir', and when asked, told him which school I had gone to. He wasn't familiar with St Barnabas but, sensibly, moved onto his next question. What did I play off? Aha! A trick question and I was ready for this test. I told him, "the grass, sir," and, still standing to attention, smiled.

Anyway, after ten minutes of all this cock and ball he got to the heart of the matter. He also asked, did I have a bank account. If so, could I write him a cheque when I would then be allowed to become a member of this old and venerable club. That I had to swear to abide by its rules, and so holding up the rules in my right hand I said bollocks. Finally, I had to repeat the club's mantra, dib, dib and dob. I was now in.

Goodwood golf was a whole different tin of fish. As a member of the Road Racing Club, I would naturally be allowed to become an instant member and to play golf on their two courses. I would be allowed to wear jeans, different coloured socks, park in the car park and use the kennel's clubhouse. All I had to do was fill in this form and send a cheque, made payable to a L.O.R.D March, for a hundred very expensive golf balls.

The lovely thing about Goodwood were the gorgeous views across the Solent and the super cute little golf buggies, called Woodies. We were now playing the golf twice a week and for a while it was all going very well. We played our new game all over the world. In the Caribbean, Portugal, Spain, Scotland, America, and Mauritius. My application to join PGA tour was declined. This was I think when my game started to come apart. For me, rejection was never easy to come to terms with. Gail's game was

totally consistent, and she kept getting good scores and winning prizes. Mine, on the other hand, was dangerous and a threat to the general public and anyone living within a half mile of the golf course.

We were playing the twelfth hole at Windlesham, one of the golf clubs where I was still a member. It's a long dog-leg right hole going uphill to the green. There's a wet, muddy ditch and a hedge running left to right, across the fairway. I skilfully hit my T-shot, so it landed short of the ditch. Gail, who was ahead of me, waited whilst I got a new club out of my bag and set up for the next shot.

What a carry on. I stood, legs apart, bottom sticking out and wiggled around as Rhino had told us do. I looked up, I looked down and remembered to relax, and so I farted. Suitably prepared, I swung the club and for a nice change the little white ball landed roughly where it was supposed to go. Golf etiquette requires that I moved my electric trolley away and stood to one side hiding so Gail couldn't see me and be easily distracted while making her play.

As usual, she made a lovely neat and tidy shot. We were walking away and looking to our balls and the next shot when I remembered my electric golf trolley. I couldn't see it and asked Gail where it was. She laughed and pointed across the fairway. My lovely Tiger Woods golf bag was now bumping along, all on its own towards the hedge and the ditch.

I think that was the last time I tried running which on this occasion didn't go well. The electric trolley had decided, without me, to carry on its way across the fairway, terrifying the rabbits and continuing onwards through the rough, bumpy grass to the ditch. It was behaving like the Duracell Bunny and just kept on going until there was a big blue electrical flash and a cloud of smoke as it ended upside down in the mud and water. When we finally got there, it was like Armageddon. I was badly out of breath and close to needing the club's defibrillator. Looking around there were bits of peanut butter sandwiches all over the bushes. There were un-lucky rabbits feet hanging in the tree and dead fish floating all around in the stream.

Needless to say, those golf clubs and bag never performed properly again. Disgusted and disappointed I gave up all the different memberships and, sulking, went off to Spain where there are no muddy ditches, and the sun always shines.

The best way to play in Spain is to join a golf society, and so we did. I got lucky and found a lovely set of Callaway golf clubs left by the rubbish bin. I gave up on my dirty, muddy, and distressed Tiger Woods golf bag and had been given a nice new one for my birthday. Re-invigorated I was all ready to restart my golfing career over again.

It all started well and both Gail and I happily played all over the Costa del Sol. As is life, things started to go wrong when I broke my collar bone while skiing and had to buy a new pair of golf shoes. From then on, uncomfortable and disabled, I struggled to play the same shot twice. I knew things weren't right when I stepped up to tee off, other players from the Torreblanca Golf Society, started to look frightened and would take cover.

For me, the lowest spot in my golfing career came about at

the Cabapino golf course, on the par three, twelfth hole. The tee box is way up on a hill looking down on the green below. It's a very pretty setting with a big pond in front of the green making it an all or nothing shot. It was a lovely sunny day, hot, with the birds sitting in the trees, watching, laughing, and generally taking the mickey.

We were a four ball, and I was the last one to hit my ball. We were all playing to win the €4 bottle of cava by playing the nearest to the pin T-shot. I did all the usual set up things like sticking my bum out, bending my knees, wiggling, and squiggling. I used my recycled, rubbish-bin pitching wedge and beautifully lofted the ball way, way up into the air.

It went so high that a Ryanair flight approaching Malaga airport had to suddenly swerve to miss my ball as it curved gently towards the green (not their fault and no one got refunded for the spilled drinks). At the very last minute a puff of wind must have pushed the ball a little bit sideways making it drop just into the water at the edge of the pond. I was so cross since I was expecting to win the nearest to the pin bottle of cava. It was a winning shot intended to go very close, or better still, into the hole. Instead, it ended up frightening the frogs by joining in with the mud bath at the edge of the pond.

We all trolled off down the hill, to play our second shots. I was focused and still determined to complete the hole in three shots. My ball was clearly visible just at the edge in the water. People tell me my brain works differently to everyone else's, which may be true. It said by whacking the ball very hard, at precisely the right angle, it would pop this little rascal out of the water, straight into the hole.

When they make a pond in Spain, they dig a big hole and line it with a really super thick, tough black polythene sheet. They then fill it with water and mud and make it all look nice and pretty. Now, getting out of it was something I'm sure I've seen done on the telly and so I got myself prepared. Normally you would have one foot each side of the ball but on this occasion, it wasn't possible because it was in the pond. So, I'm not completely stupid, and to keep dry, I put my polythene, peanut butter sandwich bag on my front foot to keep me dry and to protect my new golf shoe.

Standing in the water and mud with one dry foot in front of the ball I'm ready to go. Making the best of a difficult job, I wiggled, squiggled, and did the little dance. I started slowly and carefully bringing my golf club back for the whack-a-ball, full swing. As I did something unexpected, weird, and very strange started to happen.

Both of my new, sure grip waterproof golf shoes started to slowly slip down the plastic sheeting into the pond. From there on things quickly got out of hand. I was still standing in my new golf shoes, which had by now taken over the game. The mud slope was getting steeper and steeper, as I quickly sank further and further, down and into the pond.

There have been a few times in my life when the science just takes over and there's nothing you can do. I completely missed the ball, my new shoes jumped right out of the water, and I quite simply just fell into the pond. I came out soaking wet and covered in super stinky orange mud and bits of pond weed. Needless to say, I didn't get the closest to the pin prize, but I did get the plonker of the month award from the golf society.

Gail wasn't impressed.

Indian Takeaways

If you travel a lot with British Airways, like we do, they give you lots of grief and bundle that up with lots of rewards. It's a lot like Sainsbury's and Tesco. You get a special little plastic card to put into a drawer somewhere, with all the others you've already got. They give you frequent flyer miles (used to be called Air Miles and now called Avios). This will change again once they get a new influx of hot-shot school leavers. Collecting miles and playing that game means shopping, buying a car, paying suppliers, and whatever else it takes to increase your stash of reward points. You do it because it's just so much fun. Eventually, like with any addiction, it takes over your life and you don't want to go out anymore. It becomes like a religion.

The more you fly with BA the more frequent flyer miles you get to collect. Same goes for their 'funky' British Airways, Premium, Executive Club, American Express credit card. Their black one is like the must have, really cool, stealthy, under the counter one. It's supposed to say you're very important. The more you spend the more bonus Avios miles you get to collect. Well, anyway, the game is to spend bucket loads of money on their credit card. The reward is that they then give you a voucher to take a partner on one of their fabulous flights, for free.

Running your own company does have lots of perks. The trick was to take advantage of them. One way was to pay some suppliers, who would take credit cards, to settle their accounts at the end of the month. We used to spend a lot on toilet paper, like, who doesn't? In our case up to £200k a year with one particular company. That's a lot of Air Miles!

Once upon a time, back in the last century, British Airways were a great airline to travel with. In fact, they used to brag about being the world's favourite airline and I don't think they were wrong. These days, and in this crazy world, they are struggling to stay afloat. This I suppose is a bit of a contradiction since boats float and they are an airline? We should feel good about what, after all, is our national carrier. There is a difference. They still look good, are independent and don't receive any financial help from the government or from their union Unite. We haven't given up on them and, with our little plastic loyalty cards, probably never will.

We didn't really like curries back in the twentieth century. That's not surprising if you had ever had a 'Vesta Chicken Curry'. You just added boiling water and stirred, yuck! However, following our first trip to India and the passing of a few years, things had changed. Britain and Friday's had become national 'beer and curry night'. It was quite reasonable then, to go and find ourselves some new and interesting Friday night curry restaurants.

We always said we would return to India. Having acquired a warehouse full of toilet paper and a bucket load of Air Miles we went in search of a new, good vegetable biryani. We booked ourselves on a flight back to the capital of India, New Delhi, and on a 'see it all' tour. Nowadays things in Delhi move a lot faster than they did twenty years earlier. It's hugely busy and Indians don't understand rules. The trip to the Imperial Hotel in the city centre set the tone for the next few weeks. At the airport arrivals, we got into a black and yellow taxi that looked like it came from the 1960s. It turned out to be a made-in-India Austin Ambassador, with a Dulux hand paint job.

When our UK motorbike and car industry collapsed, the sneaky British sold all the tools and the assembly plans to the

very resourceful Indian government. They then continued to make both the same identical cars and motorbikes for the next fifty years. Instead of robots they got loads of blokes, with a box full of spanners, and a hammer to build them. They are real 'classics 'and all the Indian government departments still run these vintage Austins. You get a four-door Austin Cambridge if you're a top dog and a two-door Austin Ambassador if you're not. Elected government ministers, of course, get shiny new Mercedes-Benzes.

The traffic is mind boggling. It goes every way, up and down as well as across all the roads. It doesn't matter if it's one way or a dual carriageway. It's very exciting to see how cleverly Tuk-Tuks weave in and out of the camels, sacred cows, rickshaws, elephants, mules, and bicycles. You name it and if it moves and that includes people, then it's on the road and all going somewhere. We arrive hot and laughing at how it all works. The great thing is that no one seems to get upset, it's all perfectly normal and eventually everyone gets to where they want to go.

Despite the dodgy car with the hand paint job, we are properly welcomed. These great big Sikhs who guard the door,

blow trumpets and dance dangerously waving great big swords around by way of a greeting. Scantily dressed ladies sprinkle us with flower petals and scented water. This, we discovered, is how you should be and are greeted to any decent hotel in India.

The following day we and twelve other passengers set off on our must do, see it all tour of all the right places to go see. We meet our guide Mustafoller, Tarik Ali the Sikh bus driver, and our personal bus boy called Oy. Greetings done and off we go for the next twelve days. You have to accept that it's 25-30 degrees hot every day. India is a huge and a very crowded country of 1.2 billion people. Look on a map and you see just how big a place India really is.

Being so big and with so many people it's a country with lots of everything: industry, agriculture, architecture, history, and religion. With so many people everywhere, there will of course be much poverty and many, very poor or disabled beggars. The amazing thing is their Hindu faith, and that they are happy, welcoming, and speak English. This is still a young growing country. You must understand that it was only granted independence in 1947. With all their resources they are becoming a really modern and dynamic force. Living standards, healthcare, and education for everyone is gradually on the way up.

We do believe that by visiting a place, however poor, you are bringing and spending your money in those areas. This in the end has to filter down and to help ordinary people. In return we get the most extraordinary experiences.

We bravely stepped out, on our own, after a day's sightseeing. At the front of the hotel is a row of Tuk-Tuk taxis. Before getting into a Tuk-Tuk you always have to ask and negotiate the fare. We fixed a price with what we thought was the one-armed taxi rank captain. Having agreed the fare he tells us which motorised pram to get in. Then with his mobile phone stuck under his chin he gets in and drives us away. To drive a Tuk-Tuk is the same as driving a moped. You need two hands and two arms. Whilst talking on the phone our Captain Armless manged to do both. Drive and talk!

We spent the evening visiting the Sikh Golden Temple of Amritsar where, every day, the devoted polish all the temple's brass and gold. I'm in the cleaning business and so have a real

appreciation of what you can do with and why they still make tins of Brasso. Once the housework is done the music starts blasting out all over the site. From deep down in the most holy sanctum they bring out and carry around the jewel encrusted holy sacred book. It's like the book of the dead. It's carried along reverently by magnificently dressed pall bearers. Everyone and everything is covered in flowers and Brasso.

It's night-time and getting late when we end up in a dark, unlit part of town. To be safe we grab a Tuk-Tuk back to the hotel. We establish the price, agree I'm a West Ham fan, and we clamber in. There's two grinning boys driving, who then and for our benefit, turn on the most amazing light show and the loud crazy music. The whole of this immaculate Tuk-Tuk lights up with fairy lights, and flashing LEDs inside and out. It's so India!

Our crazy Sikh bus driver is telling us that our next hotel will be the stop over for the festival of Holi. He's very excited and stops to buy us all some coloured bags of paint powders explaining basically what the festival of Holi is all about. It's a big deal national holiday probably celebrating Ganesh, the elephant god, trampling on some kind of a demon. The night before, people drink some local home brew concoction and light bonfires in the streets to ward off the bad demons. The following day they drink even more home brew and then run around chucking coloured paint powder as well as squirting water pistols at everyone.

You are warned to dress appropriately and to be prepared. It's all a bit bonkers when at breakfast the staff start squirting you with water and throwing pinches of paint powder at you. If you go out of the hotel it's like crazy Indian paint balling with water pistols. People are running around, see you, and start chucking powdered paint at you. The water pistols create a lovely effect adding even more to the fun and mess. It doesn't stop there. People in cars and on mopeds slow down and throw it at you as they drive by.

There's even a tractor and trailer parading through town with a crew of paint fairies making sure no one gets left out. By mid-morning everyone's covered in paint, laughing, and having a great time. I became a kid again and was determined to give as good as I got, and I did. It took a long while to get cleaned up. The coach driver, Tariq Ali, gave us all a shot of celebration whisky, had one himself, and off we went to go on a safari.

All the hotels we stayed at were old palaces refurbished and renovated. There were lots of them. Back in the day there were princes and rajahs everywhere, each with their own history, little kingdoms, and palaces. The palaces were wonderfully cranky with some very strange plumbing and museum-like bedrooms. The hotel bars all had a pool table, stuffed animal heads, and skins all over the walls.

We were on a tour, so the price mattered. Down the road was the nearby Oberoi Hotel, a company whose properties we had really come to like. When you stayed there and went to the safari park with them it took longer but you went by elephant. How cool was that! No matter, for us to get to the wildlife reserve it was just different.

Early morning on our first trekking day, we had to climb up onto what looked like converted, old, eight-seater, army trucks specially adapted for the event. The trails were rough and dry. The value of the tourists' collective cameras was far more than the cost of the trucks. It was all very exciting as well as dramatic. The guides all had walkie talkie radios, and guns. I thought they were really water pistols made to look like real guns to increase the sense of drama.

We were, of course, looking for the famous, soon to be extinct, Bengal tigers. There were no bum-biting bush loos, so we were all told to go to the toilet before leaving. There were hundreds of monkeys chattering away, just like the guides and it was hard to tell the difference. Eventually the call came across the radio that

Shear Khan had been spotted across the other side of the park. Sachin Tendulkar, our driver, said we were to hang on really tight as we charged across the jungle to go find these tigers.

There were bits of cameras and binoculars rolling around everywhere as we bounced, and in part flew along. When we get to the tiger spot there were at least twenty other jeeps already there. The giant telephoto lenses were all aimed somewhere into the bushes. We were told to be quiet so as not to frighten the rare and nearly extinct beasties. The noise from the camera motor-winders sounded like a swarm of bees and someone's child needed to go and do a poo. That and the twenty jeeps arriving. ... So much for quiet!

For the tigers it was like a chilled-out weekend. Instead of working for their dinner, the tigers had ordered loads of Chinese takeaways and dinner was coming to them by the jeep load. Everyone kept going "shhhhh", which in itself sounded nosier and a bit like a dysfunctional choir. We couldn't see and so just sat down at the back of the crowd, to patiently wait. I looked over the back of the jeep and just sitting there was Tony, the biggest tiger you ever saw. I knew it to be a male as it was just licking his balls in the afternoon sun. He winked at me and said, "Shhhhh," before getting up and strolling away in the other direction.

The further into Rajasthan we went there were more and more of the hopelessly overloaded lorries, camels and farm carts filling the roads. There are essentially five traffic lanes on every road. On the left is the footpath where you overtake on the inside. Then there's the slow lane where haystacks on wheels, mopeds and camels go. Then there's the middle lane or the centre of the road. This is the kamikaze bit where everyone honks their hooters and tries to overtake. Then coming the other way, it repeats, with the other two lanes and traffic travelling in the other direction. You would think that at least people would stay on the right side of the road all going in the same direction, but that's not the way it is. Somehow, it's India, and it all works out, but I don't think you ever get used to it.

We stayed a couple of nights in Jaipur. Dinner was under the stars on the hotel roof. We were entertained by some cranky band playing on saucepans, a flute-like whistle, a fantastic Indian squeezebox, and some ancient drums. The following day we went early to the impregnable, huge, big Red Fort that reached high up into the sky. The fort was at the heart of the huge original walled city. The elephants line up down by the lake, all painted, dressed up and ready to carry you to the top of the fortress. They are magnificent and seem to be very well looked after by their mahouts. You sit up top on the seats and sway and lurch all the way to the top of the hill. It's true, elephants wear nappies. If you think cows and horses can poo a lot, trust me elephants are masters of that art.

That night our guide took us all to the cinema. Bollywood is world famous and can be fabulous. We've all seen *Slumdog Millionaire* and the fantastic final dance sequence on the railway station platform. The films are so corny and done in a special Indian kind of way. They have a domestic market of 1.2 billion people. They don't need to make movies for us westerners. The films are big on music and dance. The

costumes are great, the acting is bad, and the plots are generally the same. The customers love it.

The cinema we were taken to was fabulous as well as big. It was a magnificent, full on and beautifully kept art deco building from the 1940s/'50s. A big sweeping staircase, all polished chrome, and mirrors. In the middle of India, we didn't expect this. When people go, everyone goes, and they take the whole family. Mums, dads, grannies and grandpas, kids, aunts, uncles, and cousins. They either bring with them a picnic or just buy loads of food and pop. It's very noisy and like all good audiences it settles quickly as the film kicks off. That's where it starts to be different. They clap when their favourites come on screen, and they boo for the bad guy. They cheer when good things happen and wave their arms around to the music. It's genuinely spontaneous, hugely enjoyable and a great night out.

India is made up of

everything. It can be very hot, very wet, frozen, and cold. It can be lush green and fertile. A jungle inhabited by bears and tigers. Industrial, or just one great big, huge dessert. Our adventure rolled on into the great Thar Desert. India is never small. We arrive at this one-thousand-year-old walled fort and get dropped off at the gate leading to a tented village out on the edge of the dessert.

We're pulled along on a camel cart to the reception area where we get shown to our luxurious tent for the night. This is a bit different to the Boy Scouts camping that I was used to in the 52nd Epping Forest Scouts. We've got a bath, gold taps, luxurious linen sheets and a toilet invented by a Victorian man called Thomas Crapper (true).

Well, we have sun downers followed by the usual desert dinner of a goat, buried in the sand, slow roasted and served on a palm leaf with rice. After dinner we are invited to the clubhouse where the local prince fancies himself as a DJ. Out in the dark desert, under the stars is this beautiful clubhouse, fabulously rich and perfect. All dark reds and greens with the big, beautiful pool table in the middle. There are trophies, spears, and guns all around on the walls. Prince Wannabee is smoking a huge joint and pouring out free shots, to everyone, all night long.

Some of his very glamorous, beautifully dressed princesses rock up and the whole place just kicks off, it's party night. To be fair, the music was very good, I smoked a Cuban, and we all danced till very late. If I ever go camping again this is how I want to do it.

India is such an adventure if you go at it in the right way, and it wasn't so expensive. You could do so much and all for so little. We have so many good times and had seen so much good stuff the likes of which you won't ever see on a two-week Squeezy Jet holiday to Majorca. Of course, the other thing was that *every night turned out to be curry night!* We just had to go back again.

Gail was very impressed.

A Christmas Party?

I planned to do the next Indian trip ourselves. I contacted an agent in Delhi called Banyan Tours. They were very helpful and arranged for a car and driver to drive us on a three-week journey, west to east, around the bottom of India. Bombay to Chennai. We were very excited and so looking forward to experiencing more of what this amazing country has to offer.

We flew to Mumbai and stayed at the world famous five-star Taj Mahal Palace. This was the same hotel that Chas and Di played at and that was attacked in 2008 by terrorists who over four days killed thirty-one people. Some were very brave staff, as well as guests. There is a very sombre memorial wall inside the lobby. Sadly, it's a crappy hotel and we checked out and moved into the beautiful Leela Palace Hotel.

When it was time to leave and return home, we were very close to the airport. I gave all our remaining rupees to the toilet cleaner, and we jumped into the hotel limo for the short trip to departures. We got through the strict security and checked our bags into British Airways. They offered to upgrade us to first class for £500 which although tempting, with good sense we said no. It was an eleven-hour daytime flight. At £100 a bottle even, we couldn't get through that much Krug champagne. We'd had

enough of Sula Indian sparkling wine and so off we go to the lounge for a few glasses of proper French fizz before the flight departs.

We get to immigration, which is an odd one since we were emigrating not immigrating? The junior passport wallah flicks through the pages and wobbles his head in a way that only a true Indian can. He looks at me and says, you can't leave, your visas have run out. I know we are in trouble as we get escorted off to see big cheese wallah. India is so very bureaucratic, a legacy of British governance. We taught them how to use lots of carbon paper, make as much paperwork as you can and don't ever make a decision in case you get blamed.

I can see the problem here and argue that no harm is done by sending us on our way. The clock's running out and if I didn't do something, so was our flight. I then had one of my spur of the moment great ideas. Since I'm talking to the TDW (top dog wallah), I got my wallet out and, so he could see, was sorting through my US dollars. I then offered to pay for the Christmas party which, of course, went down like a ton of bricks. I had forgotten that they are all Hindus and don't believe in Christmas.

Why, when it was so obvious that we were white Anglo-Saxons, simply returning to our home country, stop us from leaving. Our cases were eventually returned to us, and we were chucked out of departures and left standing on the pavement. Clearly, they hadn't noticed that we were Club class, executive club cardholders. **Gail wasn't very impressed.**

We had no rupees and getting a taxi became a nightmare. Eventually some very kind and helpful Indian man swapped dollars for rupees, and we returned to tough it out on the rooftop pool at the Leela Palace hotel.

It took a week of going downtown, every day, to the government offices every morning to get granted and then pay for a new tourist visa. Once we had found the TDW, the first thing we had to do was buy a folder for him to put all the paperwork, which was about to be created, into. Having queued for a very long time we got to see the main man. I was super nice to the big cheese who explained to me that he could have us locked up as illegal immigrants. However, after we got talking about cricket (which I know nothing about!) it felt like we were

soul brothers. He explained to me that 'as the umpire' his word was final. That instead of being given out he was going to give us a fine of ten thousand rupees. This was about a hundred pounds back then.

What a relief then after going backwards and forwards for five days to eventually get the umpire's permission to leave India. It felt so good getting back onto an eleven-hour, daytime, British Airways flight. For us that turned out to be a very long flight when the entertainment system broke down.

We weren't very impressed.

Back to the Park

Having won the pension jackpot and received this promise of eternal money, strange things began to happen.

I started to get mailshots from Stannah Stairlifts. Each day would bring money off vouchers for elasticated trousers or shoes that didn't need laces. The one I liked most was a single giant slipper to keep both your feet warm at the same time. My concern was very real and one that they seemed to have overlooked. As you get older the more urgent having a pee can be. How were you ever supposed to get both feet out of the slipper and then, make it to the toilet in time, without falling over. They never explained that, at my age, falling over and breaking your hip was a serious possibility. The cleverness of this was of course they are the same company that sells the ultra slim fit, seniors incontinent pants. Something you may never have heard of, but they will pop up on your screen before you check out.

Someone told me that, when the Queen sends out all these messages of your newly found wealth, she then gives the information to Prince Andrew. He, now being short of a few bob, is very involved with age concern and on the board of so many helpful companies like Stannah Stairlifts. It was when I received a free pass to travel on buses that the penny dropped. I was getting older. I was sixty-five and the games were up.

Well, I wasn't having any of that. In fact, it came on when I was lying around the swimming pool in the gardens of our Spanish property. It was one of those out of body moments when you find yourself blankly staring up at the palm trees, silhouetted against a beautiful clear blue sky, listening to some great old music. Boom, suddenly I too had one of those epiphany moments that all the famous people keep banging on about. It was so sudden that I fell of the sunbed. In a moment of rare clarity, it all became clear as I picked myself up. I knew what we had to do.

Back in the UK we were living in a nice, but draughty old Victorian semi-detached house. Previously we had been living on a private estate overlooking the meadow of a 50-acre private park and woodland. Somehow and at that moment, it just didn't feel right, living in a semi-detached with an outside facility. We had lost our way and needed to show a bit more determination as well as ambition. There was still time.

Gail said, we had to have a house with electric gates. Not just any house, but a big bog off one. We were down a Ferrari and now having to make do with our two remaining Mercedes cars. It was a fact, life was clearly, as well as rapidly, drawing to an end. The postman was telling me and so was the government. I really wanted another Bentley before I died. I knew in this moment of pure clarity, I had to get back up off my bed and go get one.

Like everything in my life, once the idea is there, in your head, you've just got to go and get it done. So, when we got home, we started looking around for a new drum. This is a pretty miserable task. Estate agents are just such plonkers, often with silly names like Rodney, Piers, and Charlotte. They never call you back. They don't listen and really, they don't have much of a clue. They are a bit like those overweight blokes with high vis everything. Builders' bums, crewcuts, and bomber jackets. The ones who drive around on the motorways in great big Japanese 4x4s made to look like police cars. There are the ones called Traffic Enforcement Officers or Thunderbirds or something like that.

Typically, when you give someone a pair of high-vis knickers, some flashing lights on top of a look-a-like police car they become the 'mutt's nuts'. Still, you must battle on and work with what you've got, estate agents included.

We had been spoiled by living in the Manor House overlooking the Tekels Park meadow. It was so private, lovely, dark with *no* neighbours. I can't tell you how annoying it felt when living in our semi, you would go out to empty the bottles into the recycling bin. The neighbour would be hiding in the bushes and would suddenly appear and go, "Oh, hello, Robert," like it's a big surprise. I'm not allowed to discharge my licensed shotgun within fifty yards of the boundary, but the idea is tempting and just might stop them from being so bloody nice or their dog from barking.

So, I've decided that the private and gated Tekels Park is really the only place in town where successful people live. I kept popping up in the car taking a casual peek around the park. Being positive, I really believed something would turn up and of course it did. Some footballer from South America or Africa had teamed up with Shangri La Homes to commission the building of a big, bog off house with… electric gates.

Unfortunately for him Reading football club, after two brief seasons of glory, dropped out of the Premier League. The builder didn't get paid, and the footballer went back to a land where the drugs were cheaper, it didn't rain as much, and the sun shone a whole lot more.

This then was our chance. Gail loved the electric gates, which right from the start made the most terrible squeaking noise when opening. The estate agent, Charlotte, was from a local property company called Waterworks. She patiently explained to us OAPs that at our age, the squeaky gates were of course a great intruder alarm. That the in-built gate noise and the crunchy gravel would alert us to anyone breaking in at night or when we weren't looking.

I negotiated very badly. Eventually I bought the electric gates and the house that came with them for the best price I could achieve. The rooms were enormous or, as Charlotte said, were "big and beautiful" which was a phrase she had picked up from her plastic surgeon. I guess footballers must need to spend a lot of time indoors, playing with their balls.

We furnished the house from IKEA who thankfully, like Tesco and Sainsbury's, now do home delivery. Gail did a great job on the place, and it looked "right good". In part, with such "big and beautiful rooms" it was how a decent first-class airline lounge used to look, back in the twentieth century. On count back the two of us had nine sofas, four bathrooms, five toilets and nine sinks. We also had a 4.5sq metre dining room table and twelve dining chairs at our disposal. It took four men to deliver the glass tabletop. It was really big, and we could get the whole team around it.

Next on my wish list was the Bentley. It had to be a top

of the range car with dark metallic blue bodywork and cream embossed leather. Its full title was a *Bentley Continental Grand Touring Convertible to the Mulliner spec*. Wow, now doesn't that just sound amazingly exotic. Such a long way from our old Morris Minor in 1972. Interestingly that car cost us £85 when we bought it to go with our first house in Aldbury, costing £7,250.10.6d (that's seven thousand, two hundred and fifty pounds, ten shillings and six pence). The ten shillings and six pence being the stamp duty in those days. That was when petrol was half a crown (2/6d) a gallon. The telephone number was Aldbury Common 274. Oh, how I miss the last century!

I made lots of phone calls about Bentleys, even reading the trade ads in the *Thames Valley Trader*. It's a certain type of person who works in the second-hand car trade. They are definitely a different bread to estate agents. They are smart, switched on and don't miss a trick. They call you "mate" or "John" a lot and have proper names like Gerry, Doug, or Chris. It's all mobile phones and conversations can be very short. Even though I'm calling them, they quickly work out whether they want you or you're a time waster. The exception of course being when you phone a main dealer like HR Owen. Then they all have names like Miles, Bertie, or Freddy. For the price of a lovely blue, slim fit, M&S suit, and a living wage, they think they've arrived, selling very posh cars. Mummy and Daddy must be so relieved to find their third in line has finally found someone else to take them on.

When you do call, it takes a while to get transferred by Camelia, Charlotte, or Endeavour. After three or four minutes the very important Miles puts his prattuccino down and picks up. You then get to fill in a form, with the very tech savvy Miles, about who you are, where you live and what it is your bothering him about. This is because, once Miles hangs up, he will have forgotten his froffy prattuccino and go back to playing on his latest Fisher Price state-of-the-art phone, forgetting you ever called.

You can only take so much of this. I decided to send scouts

out around the empire to find the car of my dreams. It wasn't long before I was in touch with Nazir in Bradford. Now, it never ceases to surprise me, although I am delighted to be reminded that, in England, there was an age when the powerhouse of our nation was in the North. That means that there is still a lot of money floating around and that they also own and sell high end cars like Porsches, Rolly Polys, and Bentleys.

Nazir is smart, he and I are now best friends, and he has "the car of my dreams". He casually told me that this particular car was unique and had, of course, been kept forever in a heated garage. Its loving owner kept it polished and read it bedtime stories every night. So, I believed him and take a British Airways flight out of Heathrow to this far-flung town somewhere, up in the North of England. Naz meets me at the airport in a monster V8 Bentley. He called me 'mate' and burned rubber all the way from airport arrivals to their showroom. It oozed luxury and money and there were smouldering joss sticks and fabulous cars all over the place.

The one or two other 'punters' in the shop were wearing some serious bling and back to front caps. This then left me, as is often the case, feeling a bit out of place in me trainers and M&S jeans. These peeps were upper body well fit on account of their having to raise and lower their arms, answering their phones, as much and often as they do. In taking a look you see the amount of old bike chains and bling they wear. In addition, the huge watches which must cost thousands of pounds. Add all this to the weight of the *go large* mobile phones and you see what I mean. It's an all-day work out. All said and done, they were very nice northern boys showing me, being an elder, respect and called me 'bro' a lot.

Right in the centre of this circus, lit by seductive LED lighting was 'the Bentley'. Every few minutes Naz would tell me how he was best mates with Michael Bolton, a pop star. How they would go out cruising in Bradford together, etc. I politely tried to look impressed. He very kindly put Tekels Park into the Bentley's navigation, having first shown me what was also on the car's built-in television. I was so excited. It was decision time. The five-minute rule is always good in these situations. Take a moment and go to the toilet.

While washing your hands for the government decreed twenty seconds, the little gremlins inside your head start running around. They were saying "you know you want it, buy it, hurry up and get on with it". When I walked back into Toys 'R'Us Bradford, Naz being a top geezer and friend of Michael Bolton, came on with a textbook close, "cheque or cash?" Like, who has that much cash? I gave him the prepared bank cheque I had brought. I actually think he was disappointed although he did his best not to show it. It was, after all, Saturday and maybe he needed the readies to go out with Michael later that night.

He handed over the keys and paperwork. I fired up the Bentley V12 engine for the first time. In the showroom the sound was amazing. My new friends with the back to front hats, all turned and smiled. They helped opening the big glass doors and lined up to wave me goodbye. I guess it's not very often they meet white boys from the home counties. I politely waved back trying to look cool and made my first wrong turn of the day. It didn't matter, I felt like a million pounds as I inhaled the undisguised luxury of oak, leather, and polish.

Eventually I found the motorway, passing the sign that read 'Thank You for Visiting the North of England'.

Settling into the fabulous, buttermilk cream leather seat for the drive I was now feeling good. The house, the electric gates, the car. I was like an overweight Rocky Balboa running up to the top of those steps in *Rocky 1*. It was now time for the Bang and Olufsen sound system. I turned the television off and pushed the 'media on' button and guess what, Michael Bloody Bolton came out big and loud. At least I remembered who he was. The sound stuff was just amazing and that's what you get when you buy the very best. I came prepared and threw Michael into the back seat where he probably belonged. My choice being a bit more Bruce Hornsby and Bob Seeger all the way back home.

Being a bit full of it, I stopped as I entered Tekels Park, and for maximum effect put the roof down. Gail knew I was coming and was out there, polishing her electric gates. To make an entrance I dropped down the gears and rumbled noisily but magnificently into the driveway in front of our 'footballer's house'.

I knew **she was definitely impressed** since she put down her dark blue Lightweight Microfibre cloth (www.Seldram.co.uk) and once again realised she had made the right life choice, marrying me.

Crash-a-Lotti-Chef and Bike Rider

When we were last in Jaipur or maybe it was Jodhpur, I was knocked out by the sight and sound of a great old British motorbike, the Royal Enfield. All over India, from Rajasthan to Delhi to Calcutta, this was the machine of the gods. It was something that every young red-blooded Indian man aspired to owning, and many did. The 350cc Silver Bullet back in its day, was one of the best of British motorbikes. The sneaky Brits were struggling as usual and realised that change was coming fast. Around the beginning of the 1960s they sold all the tooling and necessary bits to carry on making the Royal Enfield motorbikes to the Indians. The Indians are of course industrious people and they cracked on and are still making them to this day in Chennai, a town on the southeast coast.

In India, owning a Silver Bullet is a sign of virility, upward mobility, and success. It has a unique low revving pop-pop exhaust sound when going slowly and a roar when everything was going flat out. There aren't many rules in India. You can easily get five people onto a two-seater Silver Bullet. Three on the seats, one on the fuel tank and one more on the carry rack at the back. This, of course, broadens its appeal as an Indian's family transport.

I was going through the male menopause or something. It was a life-changing time and I just wanted to be different. Having been told that the game's up and I was officially too old, this then was the next thing I was going to go and buy. I, of course, was very experienced with motorbikes having crashed and written off my first one in 1975. At that time, baby Benjamin had just been hatched. I had to go to and from work as the Chef de Partie, at the world-famous Post House Hemel Hempstead. I thought it best to let Gail have the car whilst I commuted to work on my motorbike. I'm actually not sure, having never asked Gail, if she could drive a motorbike and so it seemed like the best solution? Anyway, this worked out quite well for a long time.

For me, the worst part of being a biker was the cold winter mornings and dark nights. I had learned to ride the Honda Trail Bike on the daily commute. The journey from High Wycombe took me through the freezing and icy country roads around Amersham, Bovingdon and Chesham.

I soon acquired the essential skills, and most importantly, knew what to do when the bike skidded badly on the ice and mud. On big knobbly, off-road tyres, this really did happen from time to time. The solution of course was to jump off, roll around *a lot* and hope it didn't hurt too much.

Often the hours and split shifts would have you finishing quite late at night. On the way home at 11pm, in the dark and with no streetlights, I used to have to travel cross country. Initially it all seemed a bit scary. In the end it turned out that it wasn't all as bad as it had seemed at first. There was so little traffic that you just followed the white line down the middle of the road. The single bike headlight was about as useful as a fart in a spacesuit.

The other thing was, that if you drove down the middle of the road, you had a better chance of avoiding the lovely woolly rabbits, Bambi the deer, pretty badgers and all those other lovely little fluffy things that children love so much. People think they just sit in the middle of the road and stare in terror at a single headlight coming straight towards them. That's not true of course.

They are really quite smart. Over 100 years these fluffy little eco warriors have worked out that cars have *two headlights*. Before making their move, like Jedi knights, they just sit down calmly in the middle of the road. Quietly they choose on which side of the oncoming car is the broken headlight before making their move. I think I'm smarter than the average bear and so, by being in the middle of the road, my little brain told me I too had a 50/50 chance of avoiding the fluffy little bastards and avoiding an accident.

My first motor-bike experience was unfortunately and prematurely brought to a sudden halt. I was returning home after a lunch shift working at the Crown Hotel Amersham. It was a nice sunny day, dry and with good visibility. I had the journey back to High Wycombe down to twenty-three minutes and 46 seconds. Not quite the Isle of Man TT but I felt it was quite respectable especially for an off-road trail bike with knobbly tyres. I had my dreams of becoming a race car driver and, as a start, had bought a good crash helmet. Mum and Dad had kindly insisted on buying me some Doc Martin boots that at least had some ankle protection.

The road back from work was easy, like your favourite good-looking girlfriend. Long straights and easy curves. The best bit of the journey was when it got to Haslemere which was on the outskirts of High Wycombe. You came down the big hill into those fabulous fast and lovely long S-bends and then on up the other side. It really got your adrenalin pumping.

There was me, off with fairies as usual, thinking and trying to be like the great and good Barry Sheen. Fast into the right turn, leaning over with my knee sticking out and my Levis almost touching the tarmac. Gently easing the bike back up and then slide your bum over and into the sweeping long left hander. On that particular day, I was too busy to notice the bloody bloke in a

VW campervan. He was also trying to improve his Wycombe to Amersham time by cutting the curve and sneaking over the white line stealing into my bit of the road. Wham-bam, crash, bang, and wallop. No more Barry Sheen and no new fastest time for me. Just some broken bones like the great motorbike ace, Bazza!

I don't actually recall the moment. All I can say was that Mr Campervans wife had put down her cup of tea and come out of the back of their home on wheels. They were very concerned about me and were busy trying to pull off my now damaged, very expensive crash helmet. It took a while before I came around. They were very sweet, but I did have to stop them trying to yank my head off by undoing the chin strap. By then, thanks to all the pulling and pushing, as well as the crash injuries, I had some serious problem with backlash and the nodding dog syndrome.

Now that we were all getting along so well, I was eventually able to ask them to please take the motorbike off me as it was burning my leg. It had been a funny old day so far. What with baby Ben's night-time feasts and my getting up early I must have been tired since I kept nodding off. Eventually the good guys from the ambulance company turned up and took control. They do this all the time and opened up the back doors, chucked me in and off we went to the local hospital.

Gail turned up at Wycombe general hospital to pay me a visit, which was very kind of her. Baby Ben, as usual, couldn't care less about me and just wanted to be fed. One of the strangest things about this spectacular crash was that I had in my pocket a china, smiley face teacup. Despite suffering a severe, nodding dog, neck injury; being partially barbecued by the hot engine; flying through the air, and breaking my leg, the undamaged, happy smiley cup just sat there, on a shelf in the hospital laughing at me and my foolish attempt at a new speed record. **Gail wasn't impressed and so no more biking for a while.**

Despite my best efforts, I was unable to buy a Royal Enfield in India. To do that the bike must be sold and then road registered to a resident. Even if I could get around this then there would be paperwork issues with EU compliance and so I moved on to plan B. The internet showed that there was a dealer in Wimbledon who sold the brand new, just been made, Silver Bullets imported from Chennai in India. It had all the necessary knobs and whistles that the EU say we must have. Winkers front and back. Brakes that wouldn't lock up and skid. An electric starter and a lovely springy comfort seat. Now, not many people would know that back in the day, Royal Enfield made lots of the guns. Think the Lee Enfield rifle. Their biggest customer being the British Army and its Empire right up to and after the second World War.

It's quite easy then to see why they were so good at making motorbikes. The new bike I bought even came kitted out with ex-army, leftover khaki canvas pannier bags on the back.

I looked on the map and off we went to South London and Merton which is next to Wimbledon. It was very exciting, and I knew what I wanted. It was a done deal even before we left Camberley. It's quite refreshing to go to a bike shop and deal with down to earth and genuinely nice people. Not like the snotty car dealers with names like Rupert and his colleague called Giles. There were bikes and accessories hanging everywhere. Lots of great photos of Barry Sheen and Carl Fogarty polishing their kneecaps on the tarmac at 120mph. Then there's the unbeatable smell of engine oil.

We find Dave who steps out and says hello. The first thing you notice is that Dave has bandy legs and a limp. An ex-bike racer and a proper no bullshit biker. As usual I have no idea and

Dave helps us out with a bouncy seat and a very pretty looking paint job. Delivery is two weeks and so we leave happy. Two weeks later, Gail gives me a lift back to Merton. I had already paid Dave on American Express and scored 6700 air miles in the process. I dug out my crash helmet (like, doesn't everyone keep a crash helmet in the back of their wardrobe?). I felt that my Henry Lloyd offshore sailing jacket would be ideal for the trip back home. It's waterproof, reflective, and very tough Gore-Tex. I had some gloves and a pair of cool sunnies. Gail sets off back home leaving me with Dave, who as helpful as ever, showed me how to start the Silver Bullet. Where to put the petrol (between your legs!) and gave me some helpful tips. The main one being: Don't Fall Off!

Don't they say that riding a bike is simple and that you never forget how? So, after forty-five years, off I go. The first thing you have to do is fall off the kerb and into the road. At 200 kilos it was bloody heavy. I had absolutely no idea how heavy a fully loaded Royal Enfield was, and it was! What with all the traffic that Merton and South London can throw at you on a Saturday, it wasn't pretty. At least it got me going and in the right direction. Still, I'm feeling cool on this fabulous old retro motorbike with what looks a bit like a 1970's John Player Special paint job. At the traffic lights, I'm very aware of people looking and staring. I thought it was the cool old bike or the beautiful pop-pop exhaust sound that was getting an appreciative reaction. Then I think, just maybe I do look a bit like a lifeboatman, and they don't see too many of those in South London on a Saturday.

The excitement was soon replaced by the journey home, which was slow, tedious, and uneventful. Dave had told me to keep the speed down to 40mph for the first 500 miles whilst running the engine in. This is something you had to do in the old days. It was said this was to enable the oil to get around the newly made engine and gearbox. The gentle slow motion rubbed off all the rough metal edges and flushed out the old bits of sandwiches and crisps dropped into the engine by the blokes on the production line. Robots, of course, don't do this!

Down the A3, a fast motorway-type road, for forty miles mixing it up with lorries, buses, milk floats and rubbish collectors at 40mph is not nice. Everything passes you and at times you can tell people aren't happy at your getting in their way. After an hour and a half, I pull into the drive at home feeling like I had achieved something special. Gail was again cleaning the electric gates. She was very sweet and said all the right things. Although after forty-five years, I could tell she wasn't impressed and was trying very hard not to laugh at my RNLI sailing costume.

New toys and boys they say. I drive the Silver Bullet to work every day and gradually regain my confidence. It's weird though, that after driving cars for so long you must go back in time and to re-learn some of the 'old ways'. On a Motorbike, unlike in a car, it's very easy to enter roundabouts and corners travelling too fast. Your get-out-of-jail options are fewer. You're sitting up quite straight, and the lower speed required in the turn doesn't allow you to lean the bike over. Your natural instincts, developed and finely tuned as a mad twelve-year-old on a bicycle in Epping Forest, tell you to lean the motorbike over. Your brain on the other hand tells you that if you do that you will probably fall off. It's those moments of indecision that make the difference. So, you start to brake which on two wheels, in the middle of a turn, is never a good idea. You quickly find yourself running out of road and the curb is coming straight at you quite quickly.

Another thing I discovered was that in a car your vison is wide screen. On a bike it's quite the opposite. Because you are sitting up there in the open, with your crash helmet's narrow vison, you tend to look around a lot. It feels like you're not paying attention and that's when it's so easy to run into the back of other vehicles.

After four weeks and five hundred miles of working it all out, I think I've cracked it. It's time to go back and see Dave who wants to complete the first service ritual on my new bike. By now, and after making a lot of people laugh, I've been to the local motorbike shop and bought all proper Gore-Tex all weather black bike gear as well as a set of Wallace and Gromit, First World War goggles. It's unintentionally funny but now, instead of being a lifeboatman, I think I look more like Mr Plod on a motorbike.

Dave quickly does the business and sends me on my way with nice new oil and a complimentary air freshener to hang from the mirror? He tells me I can now 'open her up'. Now, I still don't and never did understand why or how all of us old geezers are supposed to know that a boat, car, or my motorbike is a 'she'. I think it's some old twentieth century idea that boats, cars, and bikes are a bit temperamental and like women, men don't like to be parted from them. Of course, these days, this is no longer PC or true. Anyways, I am now looking forward to the A3 Grand Prix, beating all the dustmen, the buses, the milk floats and getting back home quicker than I did the first time I made the journey.

I now manage the weekday London traffic like a pro. I'm now leaning the bike into the turns, even around the roundabouts. I'm wiggling through the traffic to get onto the front row just like all the bikers do. I was doing really well until I came upon the strangest of all things in the middle of London. I pull up at traffic lights on a level crossing without any gates. A tram rumbles across and stops immediately at right angles to the side of the road. Well, blow me, I think this is all very interesting. I thought they had scrapped all the London trams in 1963.

I'm now waiting quietly for the traffic lights to change. As I do, more and more scooters, mopeds, and bikers swarm around me all working their way to the front. This was starting to become serious. It really felt like this was the front row of the grid for the A3 Grand Prix. Many of the competitors were sponsored by Deliveroo, Dominos and Just Eat. It was all getting very noisy and hot waiting for the lights to go green. It's weird, though I think perfectly normal, that as a bloke, how stupid you can really be in these types of situations.

I'm not having any of this. They've only got *Back to the Future*-type skateboards, scooters, and Honda mopeds. I'm sitting astride the Royal Enfield 500cc Silver Bullet kitted out with army pannier bags and an air freshener. I stay focused, haven't raised my goggles which by now had steamed up. Even if I could, I didn't make any eye contact.

The goggles are a problem and they do steam up when you're not going along. However, by now the engine noise was rising. Bikes and scooters are being wound up as the combatants sensed the lights were about to change. They went to amber, and the rev counters all went to red. We streaked off the stop line and onto the railway lines. It was at that moment that the tram decided to move away. This panicked Just Eat who must have been out delivering on his very first day for the company. He glanced up, clocked the tram moving and then, without telling anyone, only went and stopped slap bang in the middle of the crossing.

In the ensuing chaos there was takeaway food skidding across the road and bikes going in every direction. With my lightning reactions, I swerved the Silver Bullet around, miraculously avoiding what would have been total carnage. Just Eat had suddenly come alive remembering his tip was based on a fast delivery time. He then performed a restart which meant I had to instantly perform another miraculous avoiding manoeuvre.

Now, Dave never mentioned that when you jerk the handlebars across suddenly, you should also let go of the hand throttle. I then found out that if you don't throttle back, the dynamic action of swerving suddenly has the opposite effect and opens the throttle of the beasty from Chennai. The 500cc Royal Enfield pulled my first ever perfect wheelie and I leapt forward into the lead. My biggest problem, apart from the steamed-up goggles, was that I was no longer pointing up the main straight anymore. In fact, I was now heading for the flashing lights on the nearby pedestrian crossing.

It was then that I had one of those MGM movie moments when everything just goes quiet and in slow motion. It's when God comes to you and tells you that things were going badly wrong. As it happened, hitting the kerb was unusually helpful in bringing to an end my first ever wheelie. Bringing the front wheel back down to the ground and bouncing the motorbike away from the still flashing yellow light. It would be lying to say that I was in control and making the best of a bad situation.

Having taken to the pavement, where pedestrians and mothers with children rule, I was now heading for this great big bush. There aren't many nice green bushes left on the streets of Merton and so I guess I was lucky. I bounced off this lovely, thick one causing it little or no long-term environmental damage. It was when I hit the wall that it hurt the most. Tough luck, but there was no time to dwell on that element of the day as the next thing to get in the way was the tree.

Now, trees are timeless, clever and have seen everything in their time. I know as I have recently read a book about trees and how they all work and talk together. This clever tree had had enough of all this nonsense. Since it didn't see any value in hanging onto me, it threw me back into the bush. I found myself still clinging onto the now bashed, crashed, and bruised Silver Bullet. Everything went quiet for a while. The Royal Enfield 500 weighs a lot more than me. So, now here I am in the middle of a busy South London suburb. Wedged in between a large tree, a lovely green bush, and a brick wall, with a 200kg motorbike parked on top of me.

Why does this sound familiar, I thought. 1975! Haven't I been here before? People are amazing and so many came rushing to help. In fact, it got quite chatty for a while. The lovely, concerned lady whose wall/tree/bush I was parked in asked if she could get me anything to help. I suppose I was still in shock and the hurts hadn't fully kicked in at that point. I hadn't had lunch and thought a sandwich, a cup of tea and a parking permit would be quite nice. As expected, it wasn't long before a Slobbovian traffic warden turned up and asked if I was going to be long? Then a police car and then an ambulance turned up.

How often do we hear that whenever we really come to need help, the first responders are amazing. They are so good and very professional in a quietly, reassuring way. They immediately took care of me and the situation even inviting a fire engine to come join the party. There was a bit of concern about the petrol leaking and needing to get me out from under the bike, out of the bush and out of the tree. Fortunately, fewer, and fewer people smoke these days. I knew it wasn't as bad as all that since the crowd was by now bored and were drifting away. Everyone, except for a priest had turned up so the signs were good.

The boys from the fire station thought it was all very funny. They hacked away at the lovely lady's green bush. They agreed with me that the bike was very heavy. To get me out they would put inflatable bags under the bike, which they did. Names and addresses were exchanged, and we all promised to keep in touch. Off I went in the ambulance to St Thomas' Hospital. The staff there told me I was basically all right. That I was covered in greenfly, had a few broken ribs which they were going to X-Ray, and a doctor would come and check me out. After about three hours I got fed up, bored, and decided to go home by train.

Getting to Waterloo station I had to catch a bus. The driver strangely looked me over as I got onboard. I was still in my full-on, but now very used 'Bike Crash Protection Kit' and clutching my crash helmet. It was like I had been nightmare gardening, covered in bits of stick, leaves and some dodgy green streaks. He was very good. I apologised and told him I didn't have any money having just had the most amazing crash. That I needed to get to Waterloo and find a train home. It was getting late by now and so I called Gail asking that she meet me at Farnborough railway station. I didn't want to make her panic and she didn't ask why I was so late or why the train station.

By this time, I hurt all over. I walked very slowly from the train to the waiting car. It never occurred to me that instead of my great big Mercedes SUV, Gail would bring her pretty little sports car. She is always very considerate and kind. Normally she won't open the roof if the temperature is under twenty degrees. On this occasion she opened it just for me since I couldn't bend down to get in. We dove back home with me half sticking in and out of the car. It was past her bedtime, and I don't think she thought any of this was at all funny. After a long day it was so nice to get home to some over-the-counter painkillers and to someone who cared and made a fuss over me.

The bike was a write off. It took me six weeks to get an identical replacement only this time with crash bars on the front.

I didn't think Gail was very impressed.

Who Needs Football?

We were now liberated seniors, enjoying our second retirement and with time on our hands, We found ourselves getting very excited about big sports games. I think it's fair to blame Thomas for this. We were wrapped up nice and warm, standing on the touchline at Wellington College one afternoon. My Mum and dad were there with us, and I had a decent Cuban stogie on the go.

Sadly, there is no atmosphere and not too many supporters. I do my best to encourage the boys when nobody else does. I get carried away running up and down the touchline swearing at the ref and shouting encouragement. I can't tell you how proud we all were when number nine, scrum half Thomas scored his first major try. I think this was also the time when Thomas realised, he was quite good at this game and could actually make a difference. We've been to a lot of club matches, concerts, school plays as well as school sports days in support of our family. I think it was the rugby, a complicated game, that got us going the most. We decided to become Harlequins season ticket holders and that by going regularly to pro rugby, we would begin to understand what was actually going on. The big attraction of Harlequins was that the nearest railway station to the ground

was at Twickenham. With no drink and driving, we could travel by train from Camberley, our home. Harlequin's ground seats 15,000 and is in the shadow of the big 85,000-seat Twickenham Stadium, home to the England Rugby team. Quins are a sellout club with great players, character, and a very loyal fan base.

I got a pair of Quins socks for Christmas and an all-weather team top and a set of gardening tools as a retirement gift from work. Gail covertly got on with buying the entire contents of the team merchandise shop. It was worth it, and she always looked good *before* the game. That doesn't always follow *after* the game on the train and on the way home. For the big England internationals, 85,000 people all seem to come by train and descend on the little railway station at the same time. It's all part of the big match experience and the rail journeys are as much fun as the game.

We take the train at our home station, Camberley, and have

to change at Ascot where they take on more coal and water. This is still, currently, a union agreed requirement to prevent the train running out of fuel. To support our sponsors, and help keep the sport going, we have time and pop into the pub for an early Guinness cocktail to get us in the mood. Getting back on the train from Ascot you discover the party had already begun in Bristol or from wherever everyone had come from. Rugby people are boozers as well as so much fun. Blokes on the way to a game are always pleased to get away from the wife and children and the wise cracks and jokes are so funny.

It's easy to get into the banter and the booze flows around freely. So much so that you just end up laughing and joining in. Rugby is such a great game, and the rivalry is never nasty. People dress up in the wackiest outfits. The train is always full up and jam-packed. The railway, and the fat controller, hasn't yet caught up with the idea that 85,000 people converging on Twickenham might just need Gordon, the *big* train, and not Percy the little weekend job.

It's a great mix of people and often you end up meeting and sharing a drink with people like the chairman of Snatch It and Run. He's on a day out with his mate who turns out to be the defence coach for Merthyr Tydfil. You never know who you're going to end up talking to. It's worth the journey even if you don't go to the match.

If you haven't been to a club game in the winter believe me, it can be a challenge. With all the keep-you-warm clobber on, the train journey is so unbearably hot, crowded, and stuffy. There's a mile to walk from

the station to the ground. When you get there, the beer's cold, the wine's cold, the seats are plastic and cold. It's in the shade, four degrees and absolutely freezing. By half time you realise you should have brought a hot water bottle, foil survival blanket, sensible boots, and anything else recommended by experienced polar explorers.

We find that getting back home on the train along with 80,000 others is tricky. It's now dark in the middle of winter and after six pints of soppy juice, (Guinness cocktails) and quite a lot of wine, it's risky. We often cheat and catch the bus one stop backwards to Richmond station which is one stop before Twickenham. That way we get a seat before the train gets absolutely rammed with thousands of very happy comedians dressed up as pints of Guinness.

The trouble is that after six pints of happiness, you have to go for a whizz quite often. It's one of those strange facts of life whereby six pints goes in and only one at a time, comes out.

That means you have to go quite often. Now the short-sighted people at Richmond station, in a cashless world, charge you 50p to use the toilet. After leaving the stadium, walking, and queuing for the shuttle bus. Then a quick, shake it all about, walk to Richmond station, things can be starting to get desperate and so can finding 50p. This can often lead to an emergency, and you then have to quickly buy another Cornish pasty to get the change to do what a man's gotta do.

Once on the train to Ascot, it is still very hot, you're all squashed in and there's no way you're ever going to get to the one and only toilet located in coach three or wherever they're hiding it. I now know this is why people leave the ground, after the game, carrying their plastic pint glasses to the station. We're OK since we've been to the pissoir, have taken off our survival gear, scarves, gloves, hats, and topcoats. We have a seat and by the time 200 more people squash into a carriage built to take 116, we know we're still going to get properly baked. There's nothing to do, you can't move because you're wedged in. All you can do is watch and listen to the comics. We often wake up somewhere we don't want to go like Tilehurst or worse still Strawberry Fields, having got on the wrong train.

Fortunately, after hours of wandering around the railway network, you do eventually get back to Camberley where there is a pub with a toilet just opposite. I know to the casual observer we must look very out of place in the centre of town on a Saturday night. The girls are wobbling around in super big high heels and next to no clothes. They wear stick-on fingernails, eyelash extensions, and enough make up that you could paint a bedroom. The men on the other hand seem to wear cheap watches, football shirts, and are just loud, smoke, and swear a lot.

Having just woken up on the train, Gail and I come wandering in. We look like sixty-year-old Teletubbies that have just come out of a tumble dryer. We're very thirsty, want to go for another pee, and are ready for a quiet drink before going to bed. It's true to say we always sleep well when we do finally get home after a game.

On one occasion, when my sleeping partner was away, I asked a friend if he would like to come along to watch Harlequins play at home. Thinking this would be man-to-man time, we would meet in the pub, take the train, and have a great boozy afternoon. The weather was good, the sun shining, and it was springtime. Have you noticed when left to your own devices everything works just fine. It's never easy once you involve other people.

I get the call, "Robert, I'm going to have to meet you there. I'm going to a children's birthday party beforehand. I will drive up in my Range Rover." OK, so out of the window goes the boozy bit. All alone I get the train and there's not much point getting there too early. Instead of the traditional pre match pints of Guinness, I start looking for my friend. The meeting point is not a hard place to find but he's late. When we do eventually find each other, he insists we grab a few beers and of course we now miss the start of the game.

He's a great bloke. A giant 6ft 8 inches tall extrovert and engages with and talks to everyone. At half time the home

team is losing badly, and we hook up with some friendly Americans, who I think were lost. Still, we all had fun, and I downed a few more pints of Guinness. Chris was driving and sensibly stuck to juices. The Americans were good value, and we agreed to meet after the game for another beer or two. Trying to keep the momentum going, and at that time, I didn't feel the need to go to the toilet. The waiting lines tend to be quite long.

So, we lose the game but do go and get another drink. No sign of the Americans. Out of nowhere, my fun buddy Chris suddenly decides he wants to go home. I had been to the loo by this time. OK, thinks I. It takes forty minutes to drive home, no problem. What I didn't know was why he was so late getting to the match. Chris had got lost and parked his 'top of the range' Range Rover two miles away on a council estate. Now Chris was, of course, still lost. He decides he is the grand master of Google Maps, and he can get us back to the car using a 'Map Jedi' shortcut. His 6ft 8 inches means he has very long legs and I'm doing my best to keep up with this Jedi Google Map Master. Off we go across one field after another, down by the river, over the railway lines and then we come to a playground. I'm now doing something like a jogging elephant that's late for lunch. One that's just been down to the lake and filled up with water. After three miles, the remaining five pints are beginning to make themselves known.

That's when surprise, surprise we bump into Chris's daughter Claire and her children. This is all very suspicious and I'm doing my best to be polite and definitely trying to not think about taking a pee. The good news was that she knew exactly where Chris had parked his car. Outside her house! Well, after a

few minutes' chit chat Chris says it's now time to go, again! By now, thank goodness, the game traffic had all gone home. Really, it's traditional after the match to go to the nearby pubs where they have both beer and *toilets*. I'm thinking OK, come on then, let's go, it's only thirty-five minutes straight down the M3, but with *no* service areas.

I've never been in Chris's 'top of the range' Range Rover (he does like to say that a lot). I know they get through petrol like rugby supporters guzzle beer. I don't think Chris is tight but, as I discovered, he does drive very, very slowly. This, he says, is to save CO_2 emissions and to save the world. Really, I ask you, who drives at 50mph on a motorway! I found it hard to keep up a conversation at the same time as trying not to breathe too much. I can say there's a lot of leg room in the front seat of a 'top of the range' Range Rover. This proved to be very helpful after the Richmond/Twickenham yomp. I was having terrible trouble in not leaking and kept crossing my legs very tightly. I am reminded as to how difficult the little children must find it when they are learning not to wet their pants when they are out in the car.

It's a smart motorway and so Chris doesn't want to stop. He is by now very concerned about his whale skin leather seats. For my part, I'm in pain, sweating and fully stretched out. I just want this all to come to an end and I'm not sure if I care how anymore. We pull off the motorway and slow down even more to 20mph. We carefully go around the roundabout and gently up the Camberley hill. I can see the end of our road approaching just around the corner. I sense this emergency will all be over in just a second. I have my hand on the door handle ready to leap out when he goes and stops at a bloody pedestrian crossing for a woman and a child to cross.

The little girl stopped on the crossing and the mummy makes her wave and say thank you to the kind driver who let them cross. I couldn't help myself and shouted and screamed at the f***ing family to get out of the f***ing road. I think Chris eventually knew at that point we were in trouble. The terrified couple ran and so did I. Straight to the nearest bush. I no longer cared if I got arrested for exposing myself to a child or for urinating in a public place.

I was a long time in the bushes and, after a while, did manage to wave goodbye to my traumatised friend. Following my outburst, he had decided it was best to just wave back and to leave me there in the bushes. I could walk the last bit up the hill to where we lived. This part of getting to know rugby had been a terrible experience. I needed a moment to recover before trekking the half mile up the hill. Like any good and practised drinker, I lay down on a nearby bench with a great big smile on my face and resolved not to go to rugby with Chris ever again.

Quins Cup Final

By being in Spain so much of the time we now miss most of the Harlequin rugby games. Because of Covid we had cancelled our season tickets and the two-thousand-mile round trip from Spain to see a club rugby game was probably a bit too much. No matter, there's a really good Irish sports bar here down on the strip that sells Guinness cocktails. It's got two floors of TV screens, banners, bunting and loads of signed Irish big game shirts. They show all the rugby games as well as all the football matches.

During 2021 we had been away sheltering from Covid and working on our new house. We were in a 'Boris style' Spanish bubble with a bunch of South American builders. We had lost track of our team, Harlequins. The 2020/21 playing season had closed. For the first time in many years, our team 'The Mighty Quins' were playing in the cup final, and we are up against multiple championship winners the Exeter Chiefs, at Twickenham, the home of English rugby.

Now here's a thing. In Spain, it's always difficult working out what day of the week it is, let alone the timings. It's either GM time, CET time or just Drinks-time. Following our Cuba libre weekend treats, lunch, and then a siesta, we had no idea what the time was. With the sun beating down, we were just having a dip in our pool when I finally decided we had got the time wrong again. 3pm in the UK is 4pm here in Spain. Instead of kick-off being in forty-five minutes time it was now actually only fifteen minutes away.

We dressed very, very quickly, put the rubbish in the car (should have done it yesterday!) and flew off down the road. No problem for Max, the made-in-Oxford Mini. He's well saucy and has go faster racing stripes across the bonnet, just like Paddy Hopkirk on the Monte Carlo rally. Max the "MIO" Mini usually goes everywhere in second gear and is really very fast. This time, however, we were on a mission to get to the game and even made third gear. Back in the 1960s Minis always did handle differently to other cars, and they still do. It's a bit spooky as we power slide through the turns. The funny thing is that, without saying anything, Gail, and I both just lean together into and through all the corners. Powering Max through the turns we set a best new time for the hill descent. With no time to stop, we executed a perfect slam dunk, lobbing the rubbish into the bin as we went flying past.

We arrived at La Calla de Mijas with the tyres smelling of rubber and the engine giving off enough heat to warm a whole house in winter. I chucked the car into the first little "MIO" Mini space getting the parking bang on, right, first time. We hurried into Biddy Mulligan's bar where upstairs all the rugby games are shown on at least six televisions. We were only four minutes late. Amazingly, Quins were actually seven points up and already storming around as if they were going to win. To be fair, expectations were low as Exeter Chiefs are an amazingly good team and know how to win a game. Juan-Jose, the bartender, quickly whisked up a Guinness cocktail and a dry white wine as we settled down to cheer our team on.

It's funny. Wherever you go in the world there is always a Harlequins supporter somewhere in the room. We were not alone. The man in the front row had on his Harlequins team shirt, was socially distanced and wearing a Quins Covid face mask. Now, we didn't know until last weekend, that Quins were even in the final. What I wanted to know was, how then did he turn up, in Spain, with all the team gear and ready for a cup final? We felt a bit underdressed but Hey-Ho, we were still there cheering for our boys!

After the last year of Covid lockdown, we were quite used to shouting at the TV and so we just carried on. The game seemed to be settling as the initial rush was over. Exeter scored a try and then blow me, they scored again. No matter, watching intensely, we both realised this was no normal Quins team. Harlequins were totally switched on and pumped up to win. The physicality and determination were so evident. They were chasing everything that moved, and every Exeter player had a target on his back.

Harlequins turned the Chiefs over and kept winning the ball away from them. OK no problem, we had lost a few lineouts and accidentally tackled the linesman by mistake. We did three things right, to every one we did wrong. As the half time approached and with only minutes left to go, the score was a fragile 14:7. We were seven points down. Really, the mighty Exeter Chiefs looked more like a bunch of country bumkins who did not know whether they were coming or going.

Out on the pitch it was like General Custer's last stand, only, this time, the Indians didn't know what was happening. The Harlequins were rampant. Our number ten, fly half and kicker, Marcus Smith, was in the sin bin for biting someone! That meant we were down to fourteen players. As the half time clock ran into the final seconds, we scored the try! – and the kick, which was worth a further two points, rebounded off the goal post. It was still 14:12 to the Indians.

The teams went off for a toilet break and so did we. Just enough time to get in some more Guinness cocktails. The country bumkins from Exeter played neat, tidy, and technical rugby. They came back onto the pitch after finishing their oranges looking refreshed and ready. By way of contrast, some of the Quins players came back on still finishing their half time smokes. Quickly, as the second half got under way, the Indians realised they were still in a bare-knuckle fight with a bunch of West London hooligans. As they kicked off and our team just kept on coming.

It was such a lot of fun. Another long-time Harlequins supporter had now turned up in the bar at Biddy's. It was quite noticeable how a hush had settled over La Cala town centre. Even the regular football supporters downstairs had sensed there was magic in the air. Showing their respect, they had all stopped watching Man United playing Swindon. They had all put their lager down, changed to the rugby channel, and started ordering Guinness cocktails. The barman, Juan-Jose, was now around our side of the bar and so was Biddy Mulligan, the 4ft 6-inch leprechaun who I think was the owner. We all love an underdog, and they too were now cheering for our team.

The Harlequins were now swapping tries with a scrambled Exeter who, despite the chaos, were still trying to play 'technical rugby'. The penalties kept being given against the Exeter Chiefs for doing things wrong. They were punched out, tired, and frazzled and the Harlequins were on fire. They pushed, scrapped, and kicked at everything. You could tell that even the ref was frightened. If Exeter Chiefs had the ball, then the Mighty Harlequins just went for it and took it. The crowd was going crazy (well, Gail, me, Biddy, Juan-Jose and the two other Harlequins supporters). We were out of our seats, clapping, shouting, and cheering at the tele. When your team is winning a cup final, you just can't help watching the clock. With five minutes to go Harlequins trampled over Exeter to take the lead.

Then, would you believe it, from the restart Exeter put one down and re-took the lead. Two minutes to go and only a five-point margin. Harlequins, still full of heart and an eye on the match win bonus, weren't finished yet. With determination and ruthlessness, they scored again and this time the Duracell Bunny Marcus Smith, kicked the ball over. We were the 40:38 winners. The premier league champions. The first championship trophy in nine years.

Outside, the clouds rolled back and a beam of sunlight from heaven shone down on the bar. All eight of us were crying, hugging and high fiving. It was just an all-time great occasion. Sure, it will mean the ticket prices will go up next season, but we can't wait to get back to the Stoop. We will remember this great game for a long time. It just goes to show what determination, heart and teamwork can achieve. Exeter played their game and wore soppy feathered head dresses, but the Mighty Harlequins, wearing DHL workwear, were just unstoppable.

Harry's Football Team 2021

Something not seen in a long, long time occurred yesterday. Frightening longboats turned up on the beaches of the Costa del Sol. Hordes of Danish people from Daneland invaded the bars and restaurants here, demanding attention and service.

Gail and I left the house early to get to Biddy Mulligan's world-famous sports bar. It's a big bar standing on a corner. This means it has two sides spilling out onto the pavement where there are TVs, tables, and chairs everywhere. We all know that Daneland is a small and warlike nation where everyone has ginger hair. What was so queer was that at Wembley there were at least 11 players and 89 Danish substitutes. No one could tell them apart. They all had very difficult to pronounce names, they were big and scary and so the officials just gave up. The 5,000 Viking supporters were already bravely battling it out with the 50,000 very excited lager drinking Brits.

Now Wembley is known as the shrine of English football. It's where the great and legendary Bobby Moore's sacred remains are buried. For those of you who don't know, West Ham and in particular, Bobby Moore, won the World Cup for England in 1966. Ever since then the bloody foreigners have successfully

 contrived to punch, bite, fowl, and cheat England out of their top spot in European football. But hey-ho, this was not going to happen tonight.

We were seriously impressed and of course always believe what we are told. The TV commentators said the entire population of Daneland were at Wembley, trying to frighten the English supporters. How come then, with hours to go, there were even more of them, here, at Biddy's bar. We understand that the Irish, like just about everyone else, never waste an opportunity to have a pop at the English. Biddy, of course, had set the place up according to the law. Weapons, axes, spears, and pointy hats were all left outside. The tables were carefully set up like a battlefield. The English and the Danish supporters were draped in their respective flags. The tables were also covered in flags. Obviously, and to obey the rules of social distancing, the Vikings' tables over one side and the English tables, the other. Already and with quite some time to go old ladies, children and local people were told to stay indoors. It was all very tense, and so was Biddy. He was worried that he didn't have enough soppy juice for everyone.

The different sides were nervously enjoying a few pre-match sherbets. As the teams came onto the pitch, people in the bar started to lose control. Them's from Daneland stood and started to chant their national anthem, whatever that was? When England's captain Harry Kane led our boys out, the English supporters responded passionately with something about God saving the Queen? The wild roar from the lions at Wembley was heard all the way here in Spain. Biddy Mulligan's again erupted with more cheers, singing and clapping.

It was a fast but positive start by both teams. The match quickly settled into a game of equals. One of the Daneland players fell over near the goal and the referee, who also had ginger hair, felt sorry for him. He told him to get up, stop crying and to have a free kick at our goal. The Vikings are very tall people. This made it very difficult for our goalie, Pickford, to see over them and they scored the first goal. Now, Pickford is a great mover from an old, well-established British family. He shouted at our bloke Sterling to hurry up and get the job done, which he and Harry then set about doing. Now, one nil down, Harry's boys were fired up.

The Danes were clearly suffering boat fatigue after the long trip rowing across the North Sea. The ref again desperate to show how he wasn't at all racist, thought they needed his help. It was forty-five minutes since they had started and so he sent them all inside for a break. After fifteen minutes, refreshed following a quick sauna and a few beers, they all came back and started playing football again. Another nail biting, bum gripping forty-five minutes passed. During this time one of our blokes must have scored a goal while I was downstairs making sure the toilets had been cleaned properly. Again, the lop-sided referee must have thought, blow this for a bunch of monkeys. It was full time, and the score was one all. He hadn't expected the game to go on this long. The deceitful Danelanders had sent the ref a case of Heineken beer for the half time break. After necking a few, he now decided he now needed to go to the toilet. He made them all stop playing for five minutes while he went and sorted things out.

Biddy's bar was getting very, very loud. Lots of cheering and the singing of some old song about the football coming home. The Danelandish showed signs of having had a long day doing what they do best, pillaging, raping and generally just being naughty. They were not so rowdy now and their team had a problem. Some of their spare players refused to get out of the sauna and wouldn't come back on to play. This in turn meant that the Daneland coach had to wake up some of his other hungover substitutes and to make them try and play football.

Our great and cunning coach, Gareth Southgate, now sent some of his spare, well-rested, sober, and finely manicured young lions out onto the park. Daneland were never going to win. You could feel the ghostly presence of the great Bobby Moore all over the stadium. Fifty thousand-plus English believers were now shouting out a traditional chant about our winning by just one more goal.

The game restarted in extra time and the ref was wobbling around and looked like he might have had too many of the half time Heinekens. Several big Danish players ganged up on our little striker, Raheem Sterling and knocked him over. That meant Harry got to have a free go at the goal. The goalie was lucky, tripped and fell over blocking Harry's first shot. Harry's no fool and seeing him lying down on the pitch, having let go of the ball he quickly decided to have another shot. BAM! The ball went straight through the net and came out the back badly injuring someone dressed up as World Cup Willy. Harry had, however, scored, and the bar went completely crazy. A glorious England team had of course won.

Gail had bought a special lucky England shirt for the occasion. Normally she would be in bed at this time of the day but not today. **Fuelled by grape juice she was seen running around the bar waving her arms in the air along with everyone else.** I, of course, being aware of my responsibility for getting her home, had quietly stuck to sipping Guinness cocktails.

Watching our national teams play is such a great pleasure. It fills up our pubs, it gets all the kids and schools pumped up and involved. People buy the shirts and little flags which they stick out of their cars. The TV coverage whips it all up into a frenzy. We need more of this and to celebrate our victories nationally.

Bullseye – Fifty Years

Much to my mother-in-law's disgust, we have somehow survived fifty years and are still married. So, to keep far away from her, I put on a big show. We travelled overnight, British Airways first class to Mauritius. Now they do treat you very, very well. They give you champagne and a dinner menu with lots of food choices using French words. You even

get given a pair of pyjamas and a pillow menu. What, for me, makes it really funny is that after the dinner and liqueurs, people actually put the Jimmy jim-jams on. Then they get into bed and the cabin staff come along, tuck you in and read you a story having first asked what time you want to be woken up, and what would you like for breakfast.

Eventually you have to wake up, shower and get ready to land. With all the cutbacks and cost savings BA no longer do first class keep fit classes so it's straight into breakfast. This time around we found ourselves in the middle of the Indian Ocean, on the island of Mauritius. No excuses, we were in a fabulous hotel celebrating our big life event, as well as avoiding Covid. Other countries seem to take it a lot more seriously than the UK and we felt very safe having our temperature checked every time we ordered a drink.

We're knocking ourselves out, soaking up the sun, lying on the beach and having the waiter bring us cold towels, fruit platters, and most importantly, rum and cokes. After a few days of all this, I do get restless and, eventually decide to 'go active'.

I'm not sure if they even make proper little sailing dinghies anymore. So much so that they have become, what I think you could safely call, an endangered species. Everyone who takes to the water seemed to prefer the Hobie Cat catamarans or the funky twenty-first century style racing boats. They're the squashed ones with no back, lots of bits of string and outriggers sticking out the sides. The trouble with both these is that they are a bit tricky and difficult to sail.

Anyways, I am no hero and after all I am a leftover from the last century. It was now time to reinvent myself and do my bit for conservation – help save the little old MIO (Made in Oxfordshire) Laser sailing dinghy. I have decided that skill always trumps size. That after ten years, plus a few extra kilos, that us old farts can have a lot more fun than the Hobie prats.

The resort where we are staying was somewhere between the

eighteenth century-named Whale Island and Serpent Rock. It was a sweltering hot day as I got ready. Baggy shorts, Panama hat, sunnies, and covered in a whole tube of factor ninety-nine sun cream. In these safety conscious times I also had to wear a face mask and a lifesaving vest that was two sizes too small for me. It then crossed my mind, was the face mask really necessary? I then wondered if fish can actually catch or spread Covid.

I was trying to look cool. At seventy-one and at 105 kilos, I think I might have failed. I waddled down the path, ignoring the all-day ice cream counter with all its lovely flavours, heading directly to the, all-action, water sports desk. The man at the boat dock had probably seen it all before. Nevertheless, he was very polite and probably being a poker player, kept a very straight face. He looked me up and down, politely avoided eye contact and didn't laugh. I knew that he thought I looked a bit strange when he asked if I had actually ever sailed before. I just said yes of course and signed his liability waiver book. There was no point in boring him with tales of the many great sailing adventures I had undertaken. Although at that moment it did feel it was a bit like hiring a car from rent-a-wreck as he pointed me to the classic little sailing dinghy made in Banbury, England.

With little or no wind at the beach, we launched the boat into the water. I felt good and with all this kit on it felt like I was in the moment and belonged here. The expert beach boys smiled kindly and gave a wave goodbye as they pushed me off. There was, of course, no wind in this corner of the bay. The boat just moved slowly, being sucked out by the outgoing tide. I thought, how nice, the boat boys were still waving goodbye to me. It finally dawned on me that they were telling me that the boat was going sideways. A small but important point I had missed! The centreboard was still stuck up and I should have put it down if I wanted to go forwards.

I was clearly a bit out of practice. Now, with the centreboard down we started going forwards. No worries I thought, from a distance I was sure I was still looking really cool. We picked up a puff of wind and started moving. I didn't think anyone on the beach had noticed anything out of the ordinary. Let's face it they had nothing else to do. There they all were just watching another mad dog English type sailor leaving port.

Now, it's never as easy as people make out. I'm a big bloke and getting your feet into the bottom of the little boat, finding the wooden steering pole, and working out which bit of rope does what, takes a few minutes. The boat started to lean over as the wind increased. It quickly picked up speed and then I remembered to let the sail out a little more. No sooner had I done that when the wind faded and changed direction. It does that when you're just in the shadow of the headland along with its fancy Turkish restaurant.

In England we call people who just sit, watch, and pass comment on us brave sailors, Grockles. There they all were, sprawled across their sun loungers sipping their AI (all-inclusive) Espresso Martinis. I kept it cool, ignoring my audience, just as a professional would have done. I quickly adjusted my position, pulled my hat down and sailed on. Without realising it, I talk to myself constantly and non-stop. I would normally think it's quite funny if only it wasn't another sign of my getting older. The wind now blew strongly from the east. I pulled the rudder across to 'harden up' (that's another funny nautical phrase!). The boat instantly went quicker and then just as sailboats tend to do, went slower.

I managed to miss all the obstacles, the nets, the fishing pots, the scuba school, and who knows what else. We went quicker, we went slower. I was being kept busy pulling on the ropes, working the steering stick and leaning right out over the side so as to not tip the boat over. All very professional just like the gold medal winning Sir Ben Ainsley would do. Time was passing quickly, and Mauritius was getting very much smaller.

I decided it was time to tackle. Can I still remember how?

Let go of the rope that holds the big sail. Push the rudder across towards the sail. Tackle and crawl around in the bottom of the boat, changing sides as gracefully as possible. The trick is getting the boat to change direction. For me, facing back towards dry land was best. All this without getting strangled or knocked out by the metal boom as it swings rapidly from one side of the boat to the other.

Well, my sticking plaster came off my big toe and the rope that holds the sail on had got stuck in the rudder's wooden steering bit. Thank goodness the "Grockles" couldn't see me. For a few moments and once again, things had become just a bit chaotic. Still, we got it all sorted out and pressed on. I think in all the confusion I had gone around in a big circle and was still heading out to sea, towards Singapore.

I had a quick chat to myself and asked the all-important question; where's Mauritius gone? I needed to change course doing it all over again. OK, so find the steering stick and get hold of it a bit quick. The little boat from Banbury has a mind of its own at times. It wanted to do the other sailing thing, which is to jibe. The manoeuvre proved to be a success. I even managed, without getting too tangled up, to get the rudder and the tiller extension all pointed together in the right direction.

Having been out on the sea for an hour I was now happy that I was 'on it'. All my old skills had returned, and we were heading back towards the land. I hadn't lost my hat or sunglasses and had manged to put the sticking plaster back on my big toe. To see where I was heading, I needed to clean my sunglasses. Doing this when you're charging along in a classic little MIO sailing dinghy isn't so easy. You only have two hands, and they are always tightly clinging onto something important. Cleaning sunglasses means you have to stick the rudder in your bottom and to hold the rope that controls the sail in your teeth.

My parents always had good teeth and with one exception, so do I. Recently I had trusted in my dentist, whose stage name was Dr Golightly (this was supposed to make you feel safe and comfortable in his care). He had told me that one of my teeth was going to give me trouble. To avoid a very expensive repair it was pro-actively better to take advantage of his special offer tooth removal. Well, let me tell you what a brutal, nineteenth century-experience that was. Having shot me full of drugs he and his assistant spent half an hour trying to get the nominated tooth out. First, they tried the mole grips and that didn't work. Then they pulled, pushed, drilled, and hacked at excavating what, given the fight back, must have been a very healthy tooth. It took both of them, standing above me on the chair, using what looked more like gardening tools, to finish the job.

I now had clean glasses and could see where we were going. We were heading to the wrong bay. I needed to make a course correction. I remembered to look around before doing anything. Looking over my shoulder there was another little sailing boat coming up alongside, a bit quicker than me. Being competitive and not liking to be beaten, I pulled in the sail a bit more to make us go even faster. Showing off, I leaned out over the side using my 105-kilo superior weight advantage. What a great photo this would have made. This is the advanced stuff that racers do in the Olympics to level the boat out. Now I was really blasting along, with the boat tipped up on its edge and me hanging out over the side, getting covered in wind, spray, spit, and dribble.

When the red mist had faded away, the challenger having met his match had conceded victory – game over. Me and the little Banbury boat had blown him away. The problem was that in all the excitement we had lost the plot and were now going where I was told we shouldn't go. It was then that I noticed the hotel's water sports rescue boat coming out rather quickly. I wrongly thought it might be happy hour. It's a five-star hotel and that after all this excitement, he was going to bring me a much-needed drink. He came in close and asked if I was all right. He told me that I was in the wrong place, that I was in a restricted area and not allowed to go there and, no he wouldn't go get me a beer.

Once again, I had to perform that dangerous tacking manoeuvre and turn the boat around. I gathered up all the bits of rope using both hands and my teeth, minus one. I sorted the steering arm out and tried to find my Elastoplast which had once again come off my big toe. It was then that I realised that there was quite a lot of water in the bottom of the dinghy. Blow this for another bunch of monkeys. I decided I was very thirsty, and I really wanted a beer. I used my lovely Panama hat, that I had bought in Ecuador, to bail out the uninvited water. I'm now missing my old boat. It's so much easier on a big forty-foot sailboat with an engine, a crew, and a fridge full of booze.

I talked it all through with myself and decided to head back to the shore. Well, that was OK and after a while we sort of got there without any further incident or challenges. We came around the big bit of rock sticking out at the entrance to the bay and curled around the headland, past the Turkish restaurant. All the grockles were still sitting there watching having now moved on to drinking Strawberry Poofs.

To get back to the dock you had to turn left quite sharply between the two great big brown boats. This was then a very skilful manoeuvre. The problem being, in the shelter of the headland, there was still no wind. In a sailing boat wind, of course, is what makes it all work. The plucky little MIO boat was now drifting nearer and closer to the two big brown boats. I decided that the only way to extricate myself from this very dangerous situation was to turn the boat around and to try again. I waggled the rudder stick, pulled, and pushed the big mainsail and succeeded in turning the boat about. There was still no wind. Slowly we started drifting away from the beach, between the big brown boats.

The "Grockles" were suddenly very appreciative of my efforts. They were now alert and all sitting up, watching critically, and smiling smugly. I drifted between the big boats towards the main beach. As I came out of the gap between these two boats, and to my complete surprise, there was a little, tiny, teeny-weeny gust of wind. After my two-hour epic sail, I was very thirsty and feeling my age. This made me very slow to respond. The boat ever so gently, went up onto its side, tipped over and sank.

The whole of the beach was made up of very happy mothers, fathers, grandparents, and children. There they were, all day long, sitting in the sun, building sandcastles, and swigging Strawberry poofs, beer, and eating ice creams. All together they let out a great big cheer and burst out laughing. Children stopped building sandcastles and were pointing towards me and giggling. Some large and very red people even fell off their sunbeds spilling their drinks. As they do, the old people just continued to stare blankly out to sea while waiting for the lunch bell to ring.

I was upside down and deeply concerned about the all-important centreboard maybe coming out. I told myself not to panic, just keep cool and come up smiling. As I surface it's OK, I still have my hat, my sunglasses and most importantly my face mask on. I climb to safety on top of the upside-down hull. I should, I suppose, have been more concerned about my bum which was now sticking out. Against my fantastic brown suntan, it was a blinder. The 'builders bottom' was like a dazzling, white, full moon rising. When I was younger my wife used to say nice things about me. She had once said that I have a lovely bum. Now, aged seventy-one, without any grace or style, I clambered up on top of the upside-down sunken boat. Modestly remembering the women and children I quickly pulled my shorts up. I managed to get hold of the ropes and to try to act as if this was all part of today's show and that I did it all on purpose. The little boat slowly, slowly turned itself back over and I fell back into the water. What else can you do?

The very nice poker-faced chap at the water sports desk, having seen all this before, came out to help in his little boat.

He so kindly suggested that it was the wind that was at fault. That it was nothing that I had especially done, and it happens to many others. He was very kind and towed me back to the beach where I was still doing my best to show I was a pro. I stepped casually over the side of the boat and immediately disappeared into six feet of water. I reappeared for the second time that day still wearing my very wet and dripping hat, sunglasses and of course my Covid-protecting face mask.

Apart from my pride everything was OK. I quickly wandered away, back up the beach, looking a bit of a mess. My shorts pockets were hanging out, the wet T-Shirt, drooping Panama hat and a life vest two sizes too small. The slightly skewered sunglasses and a face mask were now hanging down under my chin. I squelched all the way back to my wife Gail where I found her still on the sunbed. Upon my return she looked up from her book, put down her third rum and coke and simply asked where had I been and had I had a nice time? She looked me up and down and **I could tell she wasn't impressed...** I ordered a beer.

So, there we are. Our big day had arrived with a champagne breakfast by the pool. I thought by way of a celebration let's do something different. That it would be fun to take a crazy plane flight. In contrast to British Airways, I had organised that Gail

take an Air Mauritius economy wedding celebration flight over the island. It was like an old, tired jet ski with an engine tied onto the roof. It floated better than it flew. It had fairy liquid bottles stuck on the bottom of the wings, so it didn't just crash and dive into the sea. To my relief, they wouldn't take me as I was 'too big'.

For dinner the staff had set us up a romantic special table on the beautiful sandy beach. The dinner was specially made for us by the chef. We had smuggled three bottles of Nyetimber fine English champagne onto the island. The hotel put on a show, lots of un-coordinated ladies dancing and wearing tablecloths. It was a perfect day for two old-age pensioners to celebrate all the things that still hold them together: sun, sea, and booze.

They Say It's all Over (West Ham 1966)

Things in life go full circle. You start in nappies, learn to walk and hopefully do quite well. You get married, have babies, hopefully make some money. Then after a complete misunderstanding at a company conference, you end up a bit tipsy, in a bedroom with the gorgeous HR manager. You get fired and lose your job. Then your wife leaves you. The bank calls in the mortgage, she steals half your everything and you end up wearing nappies again.

We think, over fifty-plus years, we have pushed the limits all the way. Thankfully we missed out on the divorce bit. I am now in my seventies. My knees are buggered and there's no feeling in my feet. Running up and down anywhere is no longer possible and I am short of breath. My libido has gone the way of the Lilo and it's only the horizontal growth hormones that are still working.

But it is what it is, so no sense in complaining. I'm working on solutions, and I am now in touch with a professor of archaeology at the Science Museum. His initial thoughts were that I have been abusing myself and pushing my luck since I was a teenager. He's promised to get back to me soon with an invoice and some further options.

Since the boys conspired with my wife to retire me from work, which by the way has been a life-saving journey, I have had to make some big decisions.

I've given up wind surfing, especially after the mast snapped and whacked me on the head when I was out at sea. With no regret, I left my old skis and boots somewhere up on a mountain.

I recently tried to water ski behind Roman's boat on Lake Zurich. I think that either I was too heavy, or his boat needed two bigger engines to get me out of the water. I am now reminded what it was like, drowning slowly, with forced water coming out of your bum. That day, by the way, was when everyone but me, was showing off their water-skiing skills. The children will never forget and still talk about Uncle Ben's legendary run down the fifty-mile-long lake. He came out of the box, repeatedly criss-crossed the wake while spectacularly jumping over the waves.

When he heard the happy hour bell ringing over at the bar, he decided to wrap things up. He crouched down, leaned right over, and in a most determined way carved across the wake putting himself way out on the edge. To finish he cut back superfast, across all the waves and performed a fabulous backward somersault into the air and landing in the water. The grandchildren thought this was amazing and after several years, still talk about Uncle Ben, their hero. I can't compete with that and so now I've also given up the water skiing.

I always thought I was pretty good in a go-kart until recently. I discovered I was now too fat and couldn't do up the Lewis Hamilton driving suit they gave me. That it took two blokes to help me get into the go-kart and three blokes to get me out. The thirteen-year-olds lapped me twice in twenty minutes and they even scored the fastest lap. So, that's another thing I won't be doing anymore.

To keep fit I have devised a daily forty-five-minute garage workout plan. This involves going into the cold space occupied by the fridge, washing machine and water softener. Waving my arms about a lot and repeatedly trying to bend down and touch my toes without farting. The big finale to the garage workout is going out into the garden and, like a super athlete, swim in the very cold, unheated swimming pool. Is it working? Is it f**k. Apparently, it's supposed to be good for you! Although at my age, I honestly think it's more likely to trigger a heart attack. The other problem, of course, is I'm not a very good swimmer anymore. When doing the breaststroke, the front bits work just fine but, for some reason, my feet don't, and they just drag along the bottom of the pool. So, I think I've just given up swimming and to be on the safe side, sailing, just in case I ever fall in again.

Over the years I have tried my hardest and played Scottish badminton and ping-pong at whichever hotel we were staying in. Tennis to keep Gail happy. Five-a-side football in Binfield with Otto. Squash at High Wycombe with Rob. While at school I competed for the school at rugby and county high jump. I've scuba dived, flown a glider, and very nearly jumped out of an aeroplane. I'm responsible for shooting and killing loads of clay pigeons as well as a few squirrels. I was pretty much rubbish at all of this and so I have no regrets about giving all of that up as well.

We decided, once again, that a change of life was needed. Since I was having to give up so many of my life's pleasures, we should rethink our lives. Taking a ten-year view of how we would like it to run out, wasn't so daft.

The Royal Enfield motorbike and the two Mercedes cars are now gone. All that was left was my Bentley, which on its last day, was all polished and looked amazing. I drove it to Swindon to deliver it to the new owner. It was a superb day and at 100mph, with the roof down on the M4, I had Bob Seeger blasting out of all twenty-four speakers. Handing the keys over was emotional. Of all the cars I have owned, this was the best.

Sensibly and with the cost of an old people's home on our radar, we are saving hard. We sold the big old footballer's house and now live in a lovely little Oxford townhouse, right in the middle of town. It's close to Waitrose, the chemist, the pub, and the bus stop. Despite owning a footballer's house, I still can't play football although I now walk like I used too! We're now down to owning just one car, two inflatable canoes and a paddle board. We live with the River Thames at the back of the garden. Global warming and floods are a concern and so, just like Noah, we have an important escape plan.

We can only afford to take one long-haul holiday a year now. I voted to stay in the EU and so, following Brexit, we catch the Airbus backwards and forwards to Spain every few weeks. The cost of a glass of wine in Spain is only a third of the price charged in the UK and so we quickly recover the cost of the Airbus journey. So, what's not to like about Spain. The weather is better, and the people are so much more chilled and relaxed. The streets are cleaned, and the roundabouts and streets are nicely planted and looked after. The food's good and so are the sea and mountain views. The local cops are visible and helpful (so long as you're not up to no good). The shops are closed on Sundays and lunch when going to the beach is a big deal and so are drinks at sunset.

I'm not sure how any of this happened but it's been a lot of fun. Let's see where it all goes next!

A final thought.
Remember, you don't have to eat the whole elephant in one sitting.

This book is printed on paper from sustainable sources managed under the Forest Stewardship Council (FSC) scheme.

It has been printed in the UK to reduce transportation miles and their impact upon the environment.

For every new title that Troubador publishes, we plant a tree to offset CO_2, partnering with the More Trees scheme.

For more about how Troubador offsets its environmental impact, see www.troubador.co.uk/sustainability-and-community